CRIME INC.

CRIME INC.

HOW DEMOCRATS EMPLOY MAFIA AND GANGSTER TACTICS TO GAIN AND HOLD POWER

VINCE EVERETT ELLISON

BOMBARDIER
BOOKS

Published by Bombardier Books
An Imprint of Post Hill Press
ISBN: 978-1-63758-816-1
ISBN (eBook): 978-1-63758-817-8

Crime Inc.:
How Democrats Employ Mafia and Gangster Tactics to Gain and Hold Power
© 2023 by Vince Everett Ellison
All Rights Reserved

Cover Design by Conroy Accord

Post Hill Press
New York • Nashville
posthillpress.com

Published in the United States of America
1 2 3 4 5 6 7 8 9 10

My LORD and Savior Jesus Christ, Ivory T. Ellison and
Ella Wee Ellison, Dr. John Calhoun and Chorsie Calhoun

CONTENTS

PREFACE

"Finance is a gun.
Politics is knowing when to pull the trigger."
Don Lucchesi, *The Godfather III*

To observe. To question. To understand.

There is a growing misunderstanding of what constitutes a crime and who is a criminal. How many of us have peered into the mind of criminals? How many of us really conceive their motivations and how they and their methods have evolved from the prisons and ghettos of foreign lands to the halls of Congress and the White House in 2020? Where is the focus of evil in the modern world?

In *Crime Inc.*, I reveal the answer to those questions. I prove that the focus of evil in the modern world has been and remains the political Left, which now lays its head in the Democratic Party. The same political Left that birthed the Nazis who destroyed Germany; the same political Left that birthed the Communists and Marxists who have enslaved billions and murdered hundreds of millions has transformed the Democratic Party from a rabble of ignorant, violent racists to the most sophisticated criminal corporation in the world.

Consumed with pride, envy, hatred, and the psychotic need to commit murder and cause pain, the Democrats are no longer under the heel of outwardly racist and demented Klan members. They have evolved, been transformed, and are now controlled by secretly racist elites who happen to be some of the most brilliant, prosperous, and evil criminals in the world.

I wrote *Crime Inc.* to remind Americans that criminal behavior isn't just the breaking of legal statutes implemented by governments. Nazis, Communists, and Democrats are criminals not because they run stop signs or litter. They are criminals because they intentionally cause misery and death wherever they rule.

You may ask: "If they haven't been indicted for a crime or aren't in prison, how can I present them as criminals or a criminal organization?" The *Oxford Language Dictionary* defines a *crime* as "an action or activity that, although not illegal, is considered to be evil, shameful, or wrong." The taking of innocent human life; theft; the sexualization, grooming, and genital mutilation of children; obsession with pornography and filth; religious restriction and persecution; acting out in pride, hatred, deception, sloth, envy, violence, revenge, and perpetrating the genocide of the black community are all evil, and, according to the *Oxford Language Dictionary*, criminal. They are also the most successful tactics employed by the Democratic Party in its quest to gain and maintain power.

Because I know the Democratic Party well, I am uniquely qualified to write *Crime Inc.* Sadly, I was a Democrat at one time. Like most black Americans, I was trapped under local, state, and federal control of the Democratic Party for a large part of my life. Being born black in the Jim Crow South, controlled by racist Democrats, I was hunted by them my entire life. Despite that,

I have not only survived but thrived. Unlike millions of unfortunate black men who were either murdered or imprisoned by this evil institution, my intimate knowledge of the Democrats' tactics was an essential component in evading their traps and snares. This experience has made me an expert in recognizing the Democratic Party as a criminal corporation and charging it as such in this book.

I also know the criminal mind. While working for five years in a maximum-security prison, I acquired an understanding of its inner workings. During my time there, two things immediately became crystal clear: Most of the incarcerated men deserved their criminal title, and from my count, the vast majority were loyal adherents to the Democratic Party. It was also telling to find that their crimes matched the party orthodoxy. This could not be coincidental.

My area of expertise in these two areas affords me tremendous insight and credibility when discussing the criminal tendencies of the Democratic Party crime corporation and the traditional crime corporations. Deciding to compare the similarities between the two, I asked the question: Did Democrats produce criminals, or did criminals produce Democrats? Or did the laws of physics and nature conclude that they must be drawn to each other?

Observing the inmates I supervised, I concluded that the congruence of the criminal ideology of these antisocial men with the evil Democratic Party orthodoxy that dominates their lives is not coincidental. They are one.

To observe. To question. To understand.

I wrote *Crime Inc.* to confront the fact that too many Americans are reluctant to accept the fact that the evil that is protected and encouraged by the political Left through the Democratic Party is plain evil. Evil cannot be rationalized. It cannot be reasoned with. Like love, it is a force of nature without any logic or explanation. It just is. Evil people exploit this reluctance as an opportunity to cast doubt, and confusion, delegitimizing those who do have the courage to speak the truth. Jesus warned of this naiveté when he said in Luke 16:8, "the children of darkness are wiser than the children of light."

Complacent Americans—who maintain business relationships or friendships with those who encourage or practice this evil, without confronting them—are as harmful to America as the Democratic Party itself. I would remind these complacent Americans of the words of Holocaust victim Dietrich Bonhoeffer:

Silence in the face of evil is itself evil:
God will not hold us guiltless.
Not to speak is to speak.
Not to act is to act.

I wrote *Crime Inc.* to provide the reader with proof of the political Left's and the Democratic leadership's contempt and malice. The reader will understand that randomness is not at play here. The Left and the Democrats have designed a coldly calculated plan to destroy a free America and to replace it with one wielding a Godless/Marxist worldview with a wealthy, global elite that controls the strings with its Godless and Marxist worldview.

While providing security, custody, and control in that prison, I learned from the best teachers in the world how to understand the mind of a criminal: from veteran officers and from the criminals themselves. I also gained the ability to recognize the stealthy visage of criminal masterminds and their methodologies. Although this criminal visage exists minimally in the population at large, in the leadership of the Democratic Party, I find it is near universal. Democrats wield their political power to legalize and finance the political Left's criminal activities maximizing the pain of their evil actions. I reiterate, the Left's activities are not motivated by money; like all psychotics, its members covet more power for the purpose of causing more death and more misery to feed their morbidly evil nature.

Sadly, I wrote *Crime Inc.* to remind you that "the greatest trick the Devil ever played on mankind was convincing them that he no longer exists." History has proven that our refusal to believe that this evil exists is their path to victory and will ultimately lead to our doom.

The political Left in the Democratic Party is Satanic. It is organized. It is incorporated. It is evil. By definition, all that is evil is also criminal. Ergo: The Democratic Party is not just an evil organization; it is also a criminal corporation, which like the psychotics that lead the Nazi and Communist parties, is using politics as a means to maximize its pleasure by increasing its ability to inflict pain, misery, and death.

Most importantly, I wrote *Crime Inc.* to remind all believers in natural law and American values that America and the world will be saved from oblivion by we that believe in Jesus Christ and hold true to the Constitution of the United States. I lay bare the Left's and the Democrats' crimes against the laws of God and man, and their hatred for all that is good and ordered. *Crime Inc.* exposes their mission and their techniques, giving you the power of foresight and of advantage, and, thus, victory.

I hope you find it illuminating.

Vince Everett Ellison

PROLOGUE

"Michael, we are bigger than US steel."
Hyman Roth, *The Godfather Part II*

Blood drips from the chandeliers. It splatters the walls. It has even soaked through the floorboard from the ceiling to the sublevel. Hundreds of bullet casings litter the floor while fire consumes the bodies of the living and the dead. And while weak, dirty, murdering thugs celebrate victory, a once-great nation's flag is desecrated, and its honor and reputation lay in tatters. This is the scene at American consulates and embassies in Libya, Afghanistan, and Ukraine. And it is the inevitable result of delivering your government into the hands of a criminal enterprise.

Alexander Solzhenitsyn declared, "The simple step of a courageous individual is not to partake in the lie. One word of truth outweighs the whole world." I refuse to partake in the lie of the political Left. *Crime Inc.* is the word of truth.

You do not need to dream that one day you will be judged by the content of your character. It is inescapable and unavoidable. It is an absolute truth that we have always been judged by our character. Those who do not appreciate the verdict choose to deflect the verdict. Usually, racism, misogyny, or homophobia carry the blame for the character defects of the day. Those who accepted slavery remained slaves. Those who exhibited the character to rise above slavery became free either in this life or the next.

The truth: Success and excellence does not come through mankind or government. Mankind and government can only stop hurting you or "offering" to help. In you alone exists the power to excel. Your enslavement remains the government's primary goal, a truth that the political Left will deny forever. The criminal empire of the political Left has been successful beyond measure. But now we are awake. As an heir of Jesus Christ and a son of God, I am inferior to no one. Thus, the evil ones haven't any power over me. Colin Kaepernick says he is oppressed. Al Sharpton claims that he is a victim. Lebron James exclaims that he is afraid. As a Christian and a black man covered by the blood of Christ, I proclaim loudly that I am a free man. I am not oppressed. I am not a victim. And I am not afraid of anyone. These men do not desire freedom. They wish only for a larger window in their prison cell.

The first chapter in *Crime Inc.*, "A Foreign Influence," chronicles how Communists and Marxists, with foreign control, exploited the American Civil Rights Movement as its vehicle to subjugate the Democratic Party. I remind the reader that in the way traditional organized crime has migrated to the shores of America from foreign lands, so have the political criminals of the Left.

The importance of this chapter cannot be overstated. I spend a quarter of the book on this one chapter explaining how foreign Communist/Marxist governments, through patients and cunning, systematically took over the Democratic Party, thereby infiltrating the federal government of the United States.

With the intention of forcing believers to reject God, in the past sixty years, the perverts of the Left, through the courts and laws passed by the Democrats in Congress, have disrupted all of America's institutions: marriage, religion, schools, arts, business, and family. Even the Boy Scouts.

Why does the political Left hate God? Because its adherents compete with Him for power. They hate Christians because we refuse to acquiesce to their demand that we reject God, submit to their authority, and allow them to destroy our children and our culture. They hate us because we love what they hate. They hate that for us, biological women are women, biological men are men, and we teach our children the same. They hate that we love America Family and Jesus Christ. They hate the fact that their perverted lifestyle will not allow them to sire children, and we will not allow them to corrupt and sexually groom ours. Let them hate. We will always love them. We will always act in love even as we defend our families, our property, and ourselves against them with extreme prejudice.

In the second chapter, "I Will Burn in Hell for You," I argue that, like the Mafia, members of the Democratic Party belong to a cult whose influence is so complete that Democrats have replaced God as the most important figure in their lives. Christians in the Democratic Party consistently vote for people who promote anti-Christian behavior, codifying it into law while encouraging and normalizing it through public education.

I explain how the Left uses the organized crime model of operational management. Like organized crime or reptiles in a swamp, they have created a culture and environment where the lowest life forms in American society are welcomed and naturally gravitate to positions of leadership among the like-minded. Their goal: absolute power. A totalitarian state devoid of God, family, gender, or morality. They are beasts with no honor, respect, or patriotism. And they are here.

Crime Inc. explains how these Leftists usually fall into five categories: (1) the miseducated, (2) the stupid, (3) the insane, (4) the apathetic, and (5) the evil. The Stupid and the Insane cannot be helped. They must be either institutionalized, medicated, or defended against. The Evil will choose not to be saved and, therefore, must be fought and defeated. Only the Miseducated and the Apathetic can be delivered, but only if they choose to be. No one can be saved without their permission.

The Miseducated can be saved through information and the Apathetic through a sense of mistreatment or urgency. *Crime Inc.* was written to help the reader that is Miseducated, alarm the Apathetic, and identify while defeating the Evil. The pitfalls of miseducation are self-evident. Apathy, less so. Therefore, I am inclined to remind the reader of the wise words of Plato when he said, "The price of apathy towards public affairs is to be ruled by evil men." The evil men and women polluting the country have confirmed this warning.

Chapters 3, 4, 5, 7, and 8 on "The Humiliation of Black People," "Grooming Children as Recruits," "Murder for Hire," "Addiction/Dependence," and "Trafficking," reveal the Left's and the Democrats' true motivation for power: causing pain and death throughout the world. Although important to them, greed is of secondary importance, though necessary to expand their evil empire. The political Left has exploited the Democratic Party as the tool that instructs the American government to forcibly institute its values that violate even the basics of natural law throughout the world. The result has caused a global hatred and resistance to our nation that we've never witnessed before. A country once known for advancing the virtues of a representative republic and the rule of law is now known for advocating the murder of the unborn and the sexualization of small children, gay "lifestyles," and the encouragement, not the treatment, of gender dysphoria. Millions have died and are now dying through abortion, suicide, drug abuse, and crime to advance the Left's New World Order.

Chapters 12 and 13 on "Pride" and "Exploiting the Weak and Vice" explains how, in addition to spreading war abroad, the Left maintains a consistent war-like state domestically, cultivating hatred, envy, and destruction, killing additional millions. Child murder, religious restrictions, education, slavery, drugs, and sexualization and grooming of children are weapons of choice here in the homeland. The Left's strength is gained from the darkness, and its power is maintained through crime.

You will never find justice in a nation where criminals construct and enforce the law. In *Crime Inc.* I argue that every crime persistent in American culture is a byproduct of the Left's villainous nature. It's always "*them*": You can't send your daughters to a public bathroom because they may well be sexually assaulted by them. You can't have a debate on a college campus because they hate free speech; you can't go to Disney without radical indoctrination by them; you can't watch sports without protest and insanity from them; you can't operate a business without fear of being robbed by one of them; you can't watch awards shows without protest and porn exhibited by them; you can't watch movies or TV or listen to popular music or read a popular magazine without protest and porn exhibited by them; you can't send your children to school without propaganda, sexualization, and porn exhibited by them; you can't practice your religion when and where you choose; you can't keep illegal aliens out of your community because of them; you can't rear your children without interference; you can't buy affordable gasoline because of them; you can't keep much of what you earn because they steal it; you can't go for a walk at night with-out fear one of them; you cannot live your daily life without being called intolerant or a racist; you can't leave your door unlocked; you can't enjoy the summer because of riots incited by them . It is always "*them*," the Left and its control of the Democratic Party, that destroys everything that's normal or decent.

Chapters 6, 9, 10, 11, and 14 on "Stealing Elections and Corrupting Politicians," "Moral Relativism," "Exploiting a Patsy," "False Piety," and "Conspiracy" describe the techniques appro-priated by the Democrats to justify their actions, manipulate the public, and retain power at all costs.

Thus, the political Left is the largest and most profitable criminal enterprise in the world. Like a political leviathan, its filthy tentacles touch everything in this nation that is immoral, destructive, and wicked. It has not only corrupted good men and women in America and the world over but has also overturned governments, destroyed ancient institutions, and murdered mil-lions. Its attack on our first freedom, our freedom of religion, has been unrelenting and successful.

On May 5, 2022, Fareed Zakaria wrote in an op-ed for the *Washington Post*:

> For a long time, the United States was the outlier in showing that rich, advanced countries could still be religious. Since 2007, the U.S. has been secularizing more rapidly than any other coun-try for which we have data…by one recognized criterion it now ranks as the 12th least religious country in the world.

What happened after 2007? The political Left's election of Barack Hussein Obama fulfilled a forty-year goal to take control of the already-immoral Democratic Party. Its members then committed to "fundamentally transform America." They have kept their promise.

It is sad to say that President Ronald Reagan's description of the Soviet Union as the "focus of evil in the modern world" now describes the Leftist Democratic Party leadership in the United States of America. About the Communists in the Soviet Union, President Reagan continued:

> They reserve under themselves the right to commit any crime; To lie and to cheat…They are the focus of evil in the modern world…beware the temptation to ignore the facts of history and the aggressive impulses of an Evil Empire.

These traits are no longer the dominion of the now-defunct Soviet Union. They have become the property of their sole proprietor and have now been consumed by the political Left and the Democratic Party leadership. The title "Evil Empire" is now their domain. The political Left and the Democratic Party are now one and the same and are the "focus of evil in the modern world."

I submit to you and lay as evidence before mankind and the altar of history this definitive statement: If the political Left and the Democratic Party are not evil, nothing is evil.

In *Crime Inc.*, I borrow dialogue from old Mafia movies, provide historical facts, and describe essential moral conduct and juxtapose them with the actions of the current Democratic Party to provide clarity to the singularity of purpose between the two organizations.

Those who are compelled to give the Democrats the benefit of the doubt expressing the ignorant, uneducated belief that no one can be this evil, should remember that Harriett Beecher Stowe warned America about the Democrats in *Uncle Tom's Cabin*, Fredrick Douglass warned Americans about them in *My Bondage and My Freedom*, and Harper Lee tried to warn America about them in *To Kill A Mockingbird*. In *Crime Inc.*, I remind America that the Democratic Party is still an evil organization out for hire to anyone willing to pay for its services. As it was controlled by slave interests before 1865, and racist interests before 1970, it is now controlled by the Marxist/Communist sexually immoral interests of the political Left. A Democratic Party Heaven is an American Hell.

In Genesis 4:4–7, God asked Cain, "Why are you angry? If you do well, will you not be accepted?" God presented this question in an attempt to ameliorate the envy, hatred, and victimization driving Cain to murder his brother Abel. There was also a warning: "If you do not well, sin crouches at your door. Its desire is for you, but you must master it." The warning failed. Cain murdered his brother. This fratricide did not enhance the standard of his life. It, instead, saddled him with guilt, poverty, and contempt from his fellow man. *Crime Inc.* argues in the "Political Left" the spirit of Cain is alive and well.

This message is directed at all humanity but seems to be perfectly designed for the Political Left. The members of this cabal of "ne'er-do-wells" are envious, prideful, angry, and filled with hate. Sin has mastered them to a point where they cannot be distinguished from the inmates I locked in cages at the Kirkland Correctional Institution in Columbia, South Carolina.

True Christianity has been the absolute barrier to the realization of a Marxist/Communist state. For as long as people believe that the laws of nature are sovereign and that their rights are inalienable gifts from God, and the government is a servant installed by the people to assist them in securing these rights, the political Left can never succeed. Those on the left say that conservatives are full of hate and anger because we will not submit to their tyranny. We say that they are full of hate and anger because of their tyranny. Therefore, the political Left must destroy true Christianity and has chosen the perennially immoral Democratic Party as the knife to cut its throat.

The political Left has not done well. Because of its failure, like a cancer, it is cannibalizing itself right before our eyes. Few people choose to live where the Left wields power. These communities are not places in which to live but jungles in which to survive. Most are trapped. With the rioting, the burning, and the looting, it is self-evident that they hate their lives. To escape these Democrat-controlled hell holes is their dream. They envy us. Even though we love them as fellow humans, we must never become them or allow them to do us harm.

Murdering their children with federal money, stealing the earnings of their neighbors, and repressing religious observance, they shamelessly march and threaten. The inner-city ghettos and Democratic Party–controlled schools are gauntlets designed to survive, not to thrive. Where the Left holds power, there is now a new category of dying called "deaths of despair" that number approximately 150,000 a year. They consist of drug overdoses, suicides, and alcoholic liver diseases. Crime is at a forty-year high. Inflation is wrecking family incomes. The Medicaid expansion through Obamacare has led to increased abortions among the poor, as well as increased gender dysphoria, beginning with self-hatred and body mutilation, and ending in suicide among the young.

As noxious and reptilian as these people who promote these outcomes are, I must declare that no human being is my enemy. Nor am I yours. I love you all, and there is nothing you can do about it. Nevertheless, I cannot be silent while in the presence of pure evil. To be silent in the presence of this "unholy triumvirate" of government education, crime, and abortion is itself evil.

As a Christian, I am compelled and commanded by God. Therefore, I cannot fear this evil. I presently dwell within God's will, battling these forces. For this reason, I wrote *Crime Inc.* It is a continuation of a decades-long career of evangelizing and presenting hard truths, consequences be damned.

After reading this book, some of you may doubt whether there are any good people left in this world. "Guilt by association" is a common and consistent human frailty. Many Americans have met one racist white American and marked the entire country as racist but will meet dozens of good white people and not call the country good. While the government is comprised mostly of "white people" because of fear, empathy, and ignorance, many black people haven't any trouble trusting in it completely.

There is still good in this world. In *Crime Inc.*, I deal with this philosophical and metaphysical fact: If good exists, evil also exists. Whether it is the monster that murders children by shooting up an elementary school or the monster that murders them at abortion clinics. Evil is evil. There is only one difference: One form of evil is condemned by all, and the other is celebrated by the political Left.

I fight against these false prophets, principalities, powers, rulers of the darkness of this world, and against spiritual wickedness in high places. I fight against those that call evil good and good evil, who put darkness to light and light to darkness. I fight against those who cannot sleep except that they do evil and are robbed of sleep unless they cause some to fall. *Crime Inc.* will challenge you to join this fight.

Because I fight to save, not to destroy, even as I fight against these beasts, I am not their enemy.

With the political Left, there will always be something. Its members will always find something to make us hate one another and make us feel inadequate for someone else's hang-up, compounding it with the lie that if you just elect them, they will pass a law that will make you whole. If someone does not like your skin color, your sexual preference, your gender, or even your hair, they can make you whole. If you're too ugly, too pretty, too fat, or too skinny, elect the Democrats, and we'll make them accept you or punish those who don't.

It is a lie. We are all hurt. But *you* must overcome your own hurt. Government cannot fix it for you. In his holy scripture, God has revealed the imperfections that he desires we acknowledge, change, and repent. Race, gender, height, color, or physical attributes have never been mentioned. But pride, hatred, envy, and sexual immorality, the imperfections most mentioned and cornerstones of the Left, also compel us to refuse his pleas, leading us to separation from him and eventual damnation.

Ernest Hemingway said, "The only value we have as human beings are the risks we're willing to take." In fighting the leftists' ideology, I accept the risk of their wrath. If you are not one of these agents of evil, beware; they are coming for your freedom and your life. If the instinct of self-preservation still exists in you, I welcome you to the fight. I welcome you to the revolution. Join or die!

I stand in agreement with President John F. Kennedy when he said at Amherst College on October 26, 1963: "I look forward to an America which will not be afraid of grace and beauty... And I look forward to an America which commands respect throughout the world not only for its strength but for its civilization as well."

CHAPTER 1

A FOREIGN INFLUENCE

You were around the old-timers who dreamed
about how the families would be organized
based upon the old Roman legions, they
called them regimes and capos and soldiers,
and it worked. Those were the grateful days.
And we were like the Roman empire.

Tom Hagen and Frank Pentangeli,
The Godfather Part II

There are no coincidences. Things appear the way they are because they are. As a foreign power that gave rise to the American Mafia, the Triad, MS-13, the Crips, and the Bloods, a foreign power also gave rise to today's political Left. Italian influence gave rise to the Mafia. China gave ascendancy to the Triad while South America gave birth to MS-13 and the Marxists/Communists of the USSR, who, you will see, funded and controlled the Civil Rights Movement and Black Power Movements gave rise to the Crips and the Bloods.

But from whence did the influences of today's Democratic Party derive? Certainly not America. The old Democratic Party, although evil, was an American institution. But as evil as the old, racist, slaveholding Democratic Party was, this twenty-first-century version is ten times worse. We don't need to talk about what the Democrats did in the past. We win by educating the public about what they are doing today.

From all appearances, today's Democratic Party is straight out of the USSR, and since its demise, the Democrats and Communist China have become the standard-bearers for atheist/Communist thought and activity in the world. The political Left has transformed today's Democratic Party into a manifestation of Karl Marx, Lenin, Stalin, and Mao. Today's Democratic leaders are the descendants of those who are the mortal enemies of natural law, America, and mankind.

In an opinion piece by Perry Bacon written for the *Washington Post* on March 1, 2023, Bacon clarified the goals of today's "Civil Rights Movement." He wrote:

> The activists in the 1960's were quite left-wing. But today's movement is inspired in particular by Black intellectuals such as bell hooks who became prominent after the 1960's and were unabashedly anti-capitalist, feminist and radical. So the movement embraces ideas such as "abolition," invoking the movement to end slavery in calling for an end to policing, prisons and other modern institutions they view as problematic, Another key BLM tenet is racism,

sexism, homophobia and capitalism reinforce one another to prevent Black progress and therefore all must be combated.

What is Marxism? Why is it dangerous? According to Investopedia, "Marxism is a social, political, and economic philosophy named after Karl Marx. It examines the effect of capitalism on labor, productivity, and economic development and argues for a worker revolution to overturn capitalism in favor of communism." What is Communism? According to Investopedia, "Communism is a political and economic ideology developed by Karl Marx and Friedrich Engels that positions itself in opposition to liberal democracy and capitalism, advocating instead for a classless system in which the means of production are owned communally, and private property is nonexistent or severely curtailed." Ergo: Marxism is a political ideology that advocates a society with no elections, no private property, and no freedom.

In Russia, the Marxists contended that conflict stems from class differences between the bourgeoisie (the rich) and the proletariat (the worker or the poor). The Communists tried the class system in America. In the 1920s and 1930s the Communists attempted to organize poor white and black sharecroppers in the South, with no success. So, the Communists decided to substitute race for class and the elite negro class was all in. To have proximity to their white master they would do anything. Even overthrow their existing government if its replacement would force white people to allow them to sit beside them on a bus, lunch counter, or toilet. Black oppression did not exist because blacks did not have access to capital. In their minds white oppression existed because they did not have access to their white Democratic oppressors. They would start a revolution to remedy that "injustice."

Without voting, how would this change take place? The same way it took place in Russia, China, and Cuba: through the wholesale murder of millions. Who would control this system? Those who murdered the most people. How would government retain power without elections? It would eliminate free speech, guns, God, religion, parents, fraternities, sororities, unions, churches, places of worship, and anyone or anything that competed with the Communist government for power. More than anything, Marxism is a con game. Wherever it has been tried it has failed. The people suffer from lack and want, while the leaders live like kings. When the people complain they are beaten, murdered, and imprisoned. Eventually, the country implodes. Nevertheless, like a cancer infecting a new host after killing the last one, the Left will always find evil people with a sinister need for domination and power and offer them the Communist ideology as their vehicle. These evil people either infiltrated or were already members of the US Civil Rights Movement, as you will see.

Democrats are attempting to establish this system here in America. Most will never admit it. Some, like Bernie Sanders and the Black Lives Matter (BLM) organization, admit it openly. Whenever I mention Marxism, Communism, the political Left, or the Democratic Party, you must remember it is the equivalent of me saying Satan, Devil, Beelzebub, or Diablo. They are all the same.

As you will see, many black political groups masquerading as civil rights organizations were really nothing more than Communist sleeper cells financed, supported, and controlled by Moscow. After decades of historical evaluation, there is no doubt that today's black "civil rights" organizations such as BLM, the Southern Christian Leadership Conference (SCLC), the National Association for the Advancement of Colored People (NAACP), the Black Panthers, the Revolutionary Action Movement, the Black Liberation Army, and the Symbionese Liberation Army, etc., like the Mafia and Triad, as you will see, are part of the political Left and are products of illicit foreign powers.

According to Jay Richards, in a piece for the American Enterprise Institute, on February 2, 2010, even black liberation theology, the heresy that has polluted the majority of black churches since the 1960s, is a Marxist construct. Richards referred to an article by Robert D. Chapman. Chapman retired from the Clandestine Services Division of the Central Intelligence Agency. In his book *The Church Revolution*, he wrote:

Without a doubt, the Theology of Liberation doctrine is one of the most enduring and powerful to emerge from the KGB's headquarters. The doctrine asks the poor and downtrodden to revolt and form a Communist government, not in the name of Marx or Lenin, but in continuing the work of Jesus Christ, a revolutionary who opposed economic and social discrimination. A friend of mine, a head of Catholic social services in my area and formerly a priest, is a liberation theologian. He has made a number of humanitarian trips to Central America and told me, "Liberation theology is alive and well." The same can be said of its sibling in the United States.

To make it plain, the black church has been commandeered by apostate leftist black preachers to no longer preach the Gospel of Jesus Christ but to press an atheist Marxist ideology on America, starting in the black church but originating in Moscow. The proof that these organizations were never meant to help but actually hinder black people and America is evident in the fact that blacks have gone backward since the Civil Rights Movement, and these Marxist black leaders are proud of it. On October 24, 2021, the great black economist Thomas Sowell stated in *National Review*:

I have not found a single country in the world where policies advocated for Blacks have lifted those people out of poverty… I've seen policies that have led people to affluence, none of these are being advocated for Blacks in America.

A marvelous example of this fact was given by Dr. Claud Anderson. In the documentary *Contradiction*, written and directed by Jeremiah Camara in 2013, he gave this amazing statement and statistic. Dr. Claud Anderson said:

Black folks in America are in a world of trouble. Anyone that tells you black people are progressing are lying to you. You've been intentionally misled and misdirected. You've been sent down the wrong road.

We're exactly where we were in 1860 on the eve of the Civil War. You have not moved one iota in 140 years. What you are doing is enjoying the fruits from the social illusion.

In 1860 on the eve of the Civil War in this country, you only had about 287,000 black people that were free out of almost 4 and a half million. The 4 and a half million were enslaved all over America. Out of the 287,000 free black people, they had succeeded in acquiring a half percent of the nation's wealth. Now here we are 140 years later. In the richest nation on earth. You still own only half of 1 percent of this nation's wealth.

According to Dr. Claud Anderson, black Americans' economic situations have not improved since slavery. This information coincides with a June 4, 2020, story in the *Washington Post* written by Heather Long and Andrew Van Dam, stating there hasn't been any narrowing in the wealth gap between black and white Americans since 1968.

This Leftist foreign influence wrecked the black community and then deflected responsibility by telling blacks that the carnage had been inflicted by the hapless Republican Party.

White atheists/Marxists controlled the Civil Rights Movement, black clergy, black politics, black education, the black economy—and now, they control most of black life. Furthermore, the conditions in the black community reflect the conditions of the Soviet Union before its collapse. Blacks are highly dissatisfied with their condition in America, but like the Soviets and the Cubans, blacks have been indoctrinated by their Marxist leaders to blame America or the Republicans, never their leadership.

The Left's acceptance into and eventual takeover of the already marginalized and evil Democratic Party provided Marxist foreign powers, the USSR, Cuba, Vietnam, etc., tremendous influence in American politics and near-absolute control of the black community.

Like that of its fathers, today's Democratic Party's goal is the enslavement of the American people by destroying the right to private property, the freedom of speech, to assemble, to keep and bear arms, and to petition the government for a redress of grievances while including an insatiable hunger to drive God from the face of the earth. To bring this dystopia to fruition, it is collaborating with the political Left, and it is working.

The most noticeable difference between the old Democratic Party and the post–Jim Crow Democratic Party is its hatred of

God. The Democrats' former belief in a higher power, even though flawed in many areas, at least, at times, tempered their savage violence and racism while leading some Southern Christians to the light. Today, leftist Democratic hatred, violence, pride, and savagery against the American people are now unbridled.

> The Communist revolution enveloped Russia from March 8 to 16, 1917. Retaining power only in Russia was never the Communists' plan. Their plan was world conquest. As organized crime intends to turn the world into a crime state, the political Left intends to turn the world into an atheist-Communist state by infiltrating and financing disaffected groups within sovereign nations. After successfully exploiting violent revolutions in Eastern Europe and Asia, the Communists now want America. However, by necessity, they have executed a different plan in America. The American government was too decentralized and the American people too well-armed for the Left to succeed in overt violent revolution as it had in Eastern Europe and Asia. It would employ violence disguised as nonviolence. But which disaffected group would it attempt to infiltrate? You guessed it—the African Americans in the Civil Rights Movement.

A report titled "The Communist Party and the Negro 1953–1956," issued by the FBI in 1956, described Communist activities in the black community from 1953 to 1956. In the report, Director J. Edgar Hoover stated:

The Communist Party, USA, despite its concentrated efforts, has failed to attract even a significant minority of Negroes in the United States in its program. While it attempts to practice its policy of agitation and propaganda among the Negroes on a nationwide basis, the majority of its attention is devoted to those Negroes living in the Southern States. This has been particularly evident during the past year in that the party has concentrated upon organizing the unorganized workers in the South, especially those of the Negro race... The basic program of the Communist Party, USA, in relation to the Negro in the United States from 1928 to 1956 was defined in its two slogans: "equal rights" and "self-determination" for the Negroes in the "Black Belt... One of the main points in the Communist Party's program in its struggle for equal rights for Negroes in its attempt to increase Negro representation in the executive, legislative and judicial branches of state and national governments.

Does any of this sound familiar? That was 1956. The Communist Party hadn't found any traction within the black community before this time. It failed at every turn. Until...until what happened? Until it found Dr. Martin Luther King, Jr.

Understand the Civil Rights Movement was not designed to help black Americans. Or it failed miserably at its attempt. Sixty-five years after the Montgomery Bus Boycott, the evidence is clear. According to the riots of the past few years, the USA still suffers from racism, police brutality, inequality in income, education, incarceration, and opportunity.

Even the two seminal events of the Civil Rights Movement—the Montgomery Bus Boycott and the beatings at the Edmund Pettis Bridge in Selma, Alabama—ended in failure. According to Columbia University–educated journalist Charles Silberman, because of intimidation by and fear of white Democrats, "by 1963 most Negroes in Montgomery had returned to the old custom of riding in the back of the bus."

Democrats really celebrate these two events, especially Selma. According to a story in the *Washington Post* on April 11, 2022, by Emmanuel Felton, Selma, Alabama, a city of 18,000 residents, 80 percent black, is one of the poorest cities in America. Nevertheless, they celebrate. The Civil Rights Movement failed at every one of its stated goals. But it was very successful in its real intention: electing more Marxists, Coleman Young, Bobby Rush, Bernie Sanders, AOC, etc., to public office. This was the only goal that mattered.

To add weight to that accusation, the same *Washington Post* piece reported that,

> Joyce O'Neal, a retired social worker who participated in the marches as a teenager, said Selma's Black Community has never gotten what it deserved. Once the [Voting Rights Act] passed, that legislation was in place, those who came into Selma to help get voting rights just left. And we were left on our own to deal with what came next. Democrats haven't even attempted to hide it.

On June 6, 2000, C-SPAN and *Roll Call* reported that on April 7, 2009, members of the Congressional Black Caucus even got a chance to meet with their comrade Fidel Castro in Cuba. During each of these visits to the enemy of America, civil rights icon and twenty-eight-year incumbent Representative Jim Clyburn from South Carolina's 6th Congressional District, and other members of the Congressional Black Caucus, were there selling out their nation and their people.

THE MYTH OF VOTING AND CIVIL RIGHTS CRIMINALS

I have nothing against voting. But some have a false concept of what voting can do to improve their personal life. Some really believe that voting for their government representative is equivalent to voting for who will be their representative to God. They believe that this government official can entice this God to protect them, feed them, house them, cure cancer, and maybe raise the dead.

Usually, when asked to "name something the Civil Rights Movement accomplished," most people will say, "It gave black people the right to vote." Giving someone the right to vote is the same as giving that person the right to tie his or her own shoelaces. You already have the right. It need only be exercised.

Some people strategically forget that the right to vote was granted to black men with the ratification of the Fifteenth Amendment on February 3, 1870, and to black women with the ratification of the Nineteenth Amendment on August 18, 1920. History records that white intimidation was the primary reason for the absence of black voters at the polls. The right to keep and bear arms in the Second Amendment was supposed to be the cure for that ailment. However, the same cowardice that paralyzed black men when exercising their Fifteenth Amendment Rights again rose its ugly head when it came time for them to exercise their rights secured by the Second Amendment.

White intimidation is just another phrase for black male cowardice. Everyone else in America voted during Reconstruction and Jim Crow. But black men needed protection. Today the same white Democrats whose "intimidation" necessitated the black absence from the polls, through the lies of far too many black preachers, politicians, and civil rights leaders, have now convinced most black Americans that they are, in fact, their benefactors.

Civil rights leaders and Democrats act as if voting is some sort of panacea. They have convinced the black community that voting is a cure for all that ails it. Now blacks can vote. What good is it? What has voting done for them? What good is voting when you vote for the death and poison provided by the Democrats? What good is voting when you abort half of your children, kill one another, hate one another, are immoral, without virtue, slothful, inebriated, envious, and proud? Thus reflecting the very image of the Democratic Party that the majority of blacks support. Democrats and the liberals in the media and public education celebrate the Civil Rights Movement solely because 90 percent of blacks vote Democrat. That black vote has cemented the Left's control of the Democratic Party and must be retained at all costs.

With Democratic leadership, the black community has devolved and is in the midst of a mass fratricide. We are destroying ourselves while the Democrats, for whom most blacks are voting, celebrate. But, whoopie, blacks can vote! And, as long as they vote for their former masters and their own destruction, their right to vote and the Civil Rights Movement will be celebrated. Let's see how much support blacks receive from the criminal Democrats if they decide to send their votes elsewhere.

I must reiterate, the Civil Rights Movement was not designed to empower black Americans. And it didn't. It was a Trojan horse operation designed to benefit those who actually benefitted from it—mainly the alt-Left, consisting of feminists, hippies, counter-revolutionaries, anti-war activists, and Marxists/Communists. These death cults and organized crime syndicates possess the identical goals of subverting all American institutions, whether religion, economics, government, education, or family. Thus, subjecting America to the control of any Communist foreign power. Whether the power is the criminal authority of the Italian Mafia, the Central American MS-13, or Chinese Communists is irrelevant. Control is control. They are very close to succeeding.

The foreign governments of Cuba, Iran, and China have consistently used organized crime to destabilize America through the drug trade, terrorism, and human trafficking. Thus, the Leftists in the Democratic Party and organized crime have the same goals and work hand in glove.

The castration and the feminization of American men is a primary step in this strategy. The Civil Rights Movement's indoctrination of the anti-Christian concept of non-violence as opposed to non-aggression among black men—resulting in voluntary disarmament, family abandonment, drug abuse, and rampant crime—is a precursor to the castration of all American masculinity. America hasn't won a war since this assault on manhood commenced in the 1960s.

Jordan Peterson said, "A harmless man is not a good man. A good man is a very, very dangerous man who has it under control." After fifty years of poverty, prison, and death, isn't it obvious? The Civil Rights Movement did not create good men. By imbuing black men with an anti-Christian and unmanly misconception of non-violence, it was very successful at castrating most black men, making many useless, harmless, and no-good.

Non-violence is not a Christian virtue. Non-aggression is a Christian virtue. There isn't any virtue in two grown Christian men witnessing an assault of a fellow human being and not intervening because they are Christian. There is no virtue in a man allowing his wife and children to be raped and murdered because he is a non-violent Christian. Most black men allowed Leftists to persuade them to disarm themselves mentally and physically. It created a generation of stalkers, crawling, begging, and bent, who could only be pitied, not respected, and ready to choose slavery again, this time by a Leftist master. Indeed, kicking his master's ass in physical combat and choosing freedom. According to Freedomcenter.org, the great Frederick Douglass opined on this very subject when he said,

> This struggle may be a moral one, or it may be a physical one, and it may be both moral and physical, but it must be a struggle. Power concedes nothing without a demand. It never did, and it never will. Find out just what any people will quietly submit to, and you have found out the exact measure of injustice and wrong which will be imposed upon them, and these will continue till they are resisted with either words or blows, or with both. The limits of tyrants are prescribed by the endurance of those whom they oppress.

With the Antebellum slaveholding South and the Holocaust in Nazi Germany as prime examples, if history proves nothing, it proves this: Taken to its logical conclusion, non-violence ends in slavery, and death it did for the Jews in Germany and blacks in America. For he who will not defend his family, his property, his fellow man, or himself has decided to be enslaved!

MARTIN LUTHER KING, JR.—MARXIST?

After the election of President Donald Trump, during an FBI document dump of JFK files, some files pertaining to the FBI's surveillance of Martin Luther King, Jr., were accidentally released. King biographer David Garrow recovered some of these documents. On June 4, 2019, in a piece titled "The Troubling Legacy of Martin Luther King," Garrow wrote about what he found in *Standpoint* magazine. Surprisingly, in these files, the FBI claims that Martin Luther King was an admitted Marxist. One document was quite interesting. This is what it says:

> At the time King was well aware of Stanley Levinson's and Jack O'Dell's communist affiliations.
>
> The reason King enjoyed this close relationship with communists is best explained by the fact that Levinson in February 1962 passed the word to Gus Hall, General Secretary, CPUSA [Communist Party USA], "King is a wholehearted Marxist who has studied it (Marxism), believes in it and agrees with it, but because of his being a minister of religion, does not dare to espouse it publicly."
>
> Further, in March 1962 Levinson told a CPUSA functionary that King was concerned about a

"communist label" being pinned on us" but that, at the same time he wanted to do everything possible to evidence friendship toward the Soviet Union. In addition, King has been described within the CPUSA as a true, genuine Marxist-Leninist "from the top of his head to the tips of his toes." The feeling within the CPUSA at that time was, and still is, that King definitely follows a Marxist-Leninist line.

Why does it matter whether Martin Luther King was a Marxist? Since the tenets of Marxism are atheism, anti-capitalism, and dictatorship, if King and his fellow SCLC ministers were Marxists, they were not only traitors to black people and the United States of America but also traitors to Jesus Christ in the vein of Judas Iscariot.

I don't know whether Martin Luther King truly felt called to be a messenger from God or whether preaching was just the family business as his father and brother were also men of the cloth. In our Bibles, Titus 1:6–9 describes the kind of men whom God would choose to lead his church:

> If a man is blameless, the husband of one wife, having faithful children not accused of dissipation or insubordination. For a bishop must be blameless, as a steward of God, not self-willed, not quick tempered, not given to wine, nor violent, not greedy for money but hospitable, a lover of what is good, sober-minded, just, holy, self-controlled, holding fast the faithful word as has been taught that we may be able by sound

doctrine, both to exhort and convict those who contradict.

Compare the biblical description to this description of King by the *Daily Mail* on May 26, 2019, by Jack Newman: "Secret FBI tapes accuse Martin Luther King Jr. of having affairs with 40–45 women and looked on and laughed as pastor and friend Logan Kearse raped a parishioner." The FBI also wrote that he fathered an illegitimate child while married, was often drunk, frequented prostitutes, and participated in numerous orgies with his fellow pastors.

From all you have read, all you are about to read, and the two descriptions from the Bible and *Daily Mail*, you can decide for yourself whether King was in fact a called man of God.

#MLKGlobal reported on March 30, 1967, in a speech to the SCLC Board, when talking about capitalism, the system that has lifted more people from poverty than any system in the world, King sounded like a student of Karl Marx. King said: "The evils of capitalism are as real as the evils of militarism and racism. The problems of racial injustice and economic injustice cannot be solved without a radical redistribution of political and economic power."

Moreover, as the most prominent black preacher in the world, to secretly support a Communist/Marxist system that had systematically burned and pulled down churches, executed clergy, outlawed the practice of Christianity and planned to duplicate these practices in America, if true, would make Martin Luther King one the most despicably abhorrent people in the history of the world.

Therefore, it matters whether Martin Luther King was a Marxist. I was four years old when King died. I did not know him. I never met him. I do know that his image is one of the most protected assets of the political Left, the Iron Triangle consisting of most black preachers, black politicians, black civil rights organizations, and the Democratic Party. In 1977, federal judge John Lewis Smith, Jr. ordered King's FBI files to be sealed until 2027. This fifty-year hiatus gave the Marxist PR machine time to exploit America's white guilt, turning King into a national hero and icon with a national holiday, a statue on the National Mall in the nation's capital, along with streets, school buildings, awards, and statues all over America. Regarding the MLK tapes held under federal seal, we have only witnessed a small sample of what is out there, and it is devastating. When all tapes are released in 2027, all of the King iconography and mythology could come crashing down.

ALL OF KING'S COMMUNIST MEN

Dr. Martin Luther King, Jr.'s baptism into leftist politics occurred when he was introduced to Stanley Levinson by Bayard Rustin in 1956. Who was Stanley Levinson? In his piece for *The Atlantic* on August 15, 2002, Pulitzer Prize–winning author and King biographer David Garrow writes, "Levinson had secretly served as one of the top two financiers for the Communist Party USA." Levinson raised millions of dollars for the Communist Party and the Civil Rights Movement. He wrote King's speeches. He got King's book deals. He edited King's books. It was even reported by *New York* magazine on August 28, 2013, in a story by Dan Amira, "15 Things You Might Not Know About the 'I Have a Dream' Speech," that he wrote the famous "I Have a Dream" speech where King reiterated six times that black Americans were not free, planting the lie into the African American psyche that governments bestow freedoms and unalienable rights, that blacks should be ashamed of their skin color, and that our unalienable rights come from the government, not God. David Garrow also reported that Levinson gave King "astonishing amounts" of money from 1957 to 1962, the equivalent of $650,000 in today's money. All of this money, wrote Garrow, came from the CPUSA (Communist Party USA) and thus from the Soviet Union.

Understanding the political environment of that time, for Martin Luther King to knowingly collaborate with the Communists and their number one financier in founding, bankrolling, and controlling the SCLC is the equivalent to Al Sharpton having the National Action Network organized, bankrolled, and controlled by Al-Qaeda, ISIS, and the Taliban.

The USSR and the United States were engaged in a Cold War death fight for world domination, with nation-states, nuclear weapons, the CIA, KGB, trillions of dollars, and billions of lives involved. There were no spectators in this fight. Everyone had to choose a side. The US Department of Justice believed that King chose the Communists. King was in over his head.

Stanley Levinson was said to be King's closest white friend. Nevertheless, the most excellent piece of existing evidence proving sinister intent behind the relationship between the preacher and the Communist is that there is no recording of King ever being seen with Levinson or ever mentioning his name in public. Levinson was not seen at any of the marches or speeches, or meetings at the White House. He only met with and talked to King alone in secret or with fellow Communists. He did not end up with Martin Luther King by accident. Stanley Levinson was an operative. He was a ghost, but the government knew all about him.

Levinson's danger was to such an extreme that in 1984 when fellow Pulitzer Prize–winning author and King biographer Taylor Branch requested documents from the FBI verifying its contention that Levinson had been a top-level Communist agent, the justice department argued in federal court that the release of thirty- to thirty-five-year-old informant reports on Levinson would damage national security.

Page 836 of *Parting the Waters* by Taylor Branch intimated that Levinson's control over Martin Luther King was so absolute that after many warnings from Attorney General Robert Kennedy and President John F. Kennedy about Levinson's ties to the Communists in the USSR and Levinson's intent to use the Civil Rights Movement to hurt America, King still refused to sever ties with Levinson even after personally promising the president that he would do so.

Taylor Branch writes on page 692 of *Parting the Waters* that King had become so corrupted by Levinson and the Communists that in 1963 King himself was designated by the FBI as an enemy of the United States. Branch writes:

> They (The FBI) had snared King in a nest of spies. The Dorchester meeting might as well have occurred in Red Square... "I see no further need to contacting Rev. King inasmuch as he obviously does not desire to be given the truth," (Deke) Deloach concluded. "The fact that he is a vicious liar is amply demonstrated by the fact he constantly associates with and takes instructions from Stanley Levinson who is a hidden member of the Communist Party in New York." "I concur," Hoover scrawled at the bottom of the

memo. With that, on King's 34th birthday the FBI officially wrote him off as unfit for mediation or negotiation. Thereafter, upon receiving intelligence that someone was trying to kill him, the Bureau would refuse to warn King as it routinely warned other potential targets such as Shuttlesworth. The FBI assigned full enemy status to King.

This is fascinating! On page 209 of this same book, Branch wrote that in 1956, the year that Levinson met King, the Communist Party in Moscow ordered its agents in the Civil Rights Movement to establish a "separate national development for American Negroes, modeled on the Soviet Republics." Thus, through the Civil Rights Movement, the Communist Party of the USSR was about to take over the black community. And with millions of new black votes and the money of the white liberals controlling the Civil Rights Movement, the atheists/Marxists would take over the already-evil Democratic Party, entrench themselves into it, and dominate our national politics for the next sixty years.

Like organized crime, the motivations of the Confederates and the members of the political Left are secretive and covert. They betray, lie, plot, connive, and seduce. They claim to love democracy when their primary goal is its destruction. They claim to have the best interest of the black community at heart when the black community is nothing more than suicide bombers in their quest for world domination.

Thankfully, the FBI in the 1960s was not very trusting. While Martin Luther King denied Communist membership and any Communist affiliations, through wiretaps authorized by fellow liberal icon Robert Kennedy, the FBI knew that King was lying.

Highlighting this point, King biographer David Garrow, in a piece for *Standpoint* magazine, wrote:

> Stanley D. Levinson was a "secret member" of the Communist Party USA (CPUSA). Kennedy's aides and finally, his brother, the President of the United States—warned King to cease contact with Levinson, but King's promised compliance was dissembling, he and Levinson communicated indirectly through another attorney, Clarence Jones, who, like Levinson was himself already being wiretapped by the FBI. Presented with evidence of King's duplicity, plus FBI claims that King had told Levinson that he was a Marxist, a reluctant Attorney General approved the FBI's request to place King under direct surveillance.

Marxism and atheism are synonymous. One cannot exist without the other. Martin Luther King knew this. He knew that the tenets of capitalism derived from the Christian doctrine of "sowing and reaping." In Marxist theory, it is understood that no Christian people would knowingly turn to an atheist/Marxist government. The transformation must occur through seduction, lies, and coercion. It has worked splendidly. On May 29, 2019, a FiveThirtyEight story headlined "Democrats Have Gotten A Lot Less Religious, Why Democrats Struggle to Mobilize a Religious Left" states:

> [T]he share of the people in the Democratic coalition who don't identify with any religion doubled, from 14 percent in 1998 to 28 percent in 2018, according to the General Social Survey.

The Republicans record 84 percent identify with a religion. The result is that today's Democratic Party is increasingly secular.

When you include the fact that black people, who make up about 23 percent of the Democratic Party electorate, are religious in name only, as they do not reflect it in their voting, you can surmise how the Democratic Party has turned into an atheist organization, just as the Communists envisioned.

Indeed, in his September 13, 2022, piece for the *Washington Post* titled "U.S. Christian majority could fade in coming decades, models find," Bob Smietana says:

> If current trends continue, Christians could make up less than half of the population—as little as a third—in 50 years. Those are among the major findings of a new report from Pew regarding the United States' religious future, a future in which Christianity, though diminished, persists while non-Christian faiths grow amid rising secularization.

Although one can rehabilitate people, one cannot rehabilitate evil. People are not evil. Ideas and actions are evil, and they are forever fixed. The Marxist/Communist ideology is an evil ideology. It is evil because it seeks to drive God from the face of the earth. In an August 29, 2019, *Wall Street Journal* opinion piece, Marion Smith correctly said, "An atheistic ideology, communism is not only irreligious but antireligious."

In the decades since Martin Luther King turned the black church over to the Marxists, black church attendance has suffered the most. In his 2018 doctoral dissertation titled "The Decline of Church Attendance in America: A Biblical Mandate for Black Males to Godly Leadership," Elder E.Q. Truss wrote: "Studies show for several decades church attendance declined in Baptist churches across America by 61 percent."

On May 26, 2021, a new study reported by Religious News Service reported:

> A new study from Lifeway Research suggests more Protestant churches closed in 2019 than opened continuing a decade's long slide that is only expected to accelerate...4,500 churches closed while about 3,000 new congregations were started.

People go to church to commune with God and touch the divine. Instead, they get a Sunday morning disco fashion show. They experience the things they experience daily in society. They cannot touch the divine because it is now more political than it is spiritual. A Democratic Party–controlled black church cannot speak for God because the Marxist apostate black preachers that control most congregations will not speak on the sins of abortion, LGBTQ lifestyles, divorce, fornication, drug abuse, godless education, and the fact that his congregation should not be voting for those politicians that support them.

Most of these black preachers speak of envy, oppression, white privilege, and the lie that one can buy salvation and earthly wealth by tithing. They do not speak of repentance, love, forgiveness, forbearance, and reconciliation. Like a starving customer leaving a restaurant after an expensive meal, the congregants know whether they have been adequately fed. They know if they've been satisfied. They know whether they've been touched by the Holy Spirit.

The Marxist ideology of civil rights politics intertwined with the Marxist Black Lives Matter (BLM) organization will never fulfill the needs of a tortured soul seeking the salvation of Jesus Christ.

Like taking the knife from a psychotic and providing him with a machine gun, the Communists made an already evil Democratic Party eviler. The majority of the American public would have rejected everything the Communists espoused. But being the oldest political party in the modern world, the Democratic Party would lend its credibility to Communists. Already a party dripping with the blood of innocents, Democrats are willing to lie in an effective scheme to seduce Americans into the death cult of Marxism. By 1960, for over 160 years, the Democratic Party leadership had demonstrated that it was willing to kill, betray, or corrupt anyone for absolute power.

In "Rules for Radicals," Saul Alinsky advised young Marxists who were expelled from the 1968 Democratic Party Convention because they were not delegates to "become the delegates." They took his advice. These 1960s outcasts are now the party's standard bearers. They had found fertile ground to sow their seeds of death. And the blood of the weak and the innocent would be their irrigation.

But before the Marxists/Communists could corrupt black American culture, they needed to corrupt America's institutions. Andrew Breitbart once said, "Politics is downstream from culture." All black culture rests in the black church. Here Martin Luther King would prove indispensable.

The Democratic Party had no intention of using "love and high-mindedness." It used force, and because of this, it has failed in all of its spoken objectives of ending poverty, crime, despair, and equality. Nevertheless, it has succeeded wildly in its primary and dual objective with organized crime: electing Marxists by exploiting the black vote for power and control.

But why did Communists promise integration and civil rights to American blacks? Did they really care about the welfare of black Americans? Of course not. Like organized criminals, Communists are only concerned with themselves. Organized crime has known for centuries that giving people what they want—especially if it is illegal, addictive, and evil—is the fastest and surest way of gaining money and power. Segments of the population were lured to the inescapable trap of organized crime through drugs, gambling, prostitution, and porn through this one absolute fact. Members of the political Left themselves, being members of organized crime, employed these tactics to perfection.

Equality and forced integration with their former masters would be the crack cocaine that would lead many black Americans into the trap of the political Left. The promise of using the bathroom and eating a hamburger beside their former white masters was enough to not only entice some blacks to join the political Left but also to take beatings, jailing, and death for them.

Furthermore, just as the Mafia never intends for one of its victims to ever pay off a debt, break an addiction, or stop frequenting a whore house, the political Left never intends to give inferior-minded black Americans the integration and equality they most desire because it can't. Like the donkey chasing the carrot at the end of a pole, the Left's plan is designed to keep you working for its benefit while you spend your entire life chasing an illusion.

Operations that overturn the social order of a great and powerful nation do not spring up organically. They are funded. They are organized. People are trained, and operatives are recruited. The epicenter of activity and training for operatives in the Civil Rights Movement was a school founded in 1932 in the hills of

Monteagle, Tennessee, in Grundy County, called Highlander Folk School. Highlander Folk School was designated as a Communist training camp on US soil whose charter was revoked and property was confiscated by the state of Tennessee in 1961.

The school was co-founded and administered by three white "suspected" Communists, Donald Lee West, Myles Horton, and James Dombrowski. "Suspected" because these Communists learned from their mentors in organized crime how to protect themselves from responsibility by taking the "Fifth" and never admitting to their genuine affiliations. No matter the evidence, deny, deny, deny your true intentions and affiliations. This is the mantra of organized crime and liberal Democrats (but I'm being redundant). No matter the evidence presented, Donald Lee West, Myles Horton, James Dombrowski, and Stanley Levinson always denied that they were Communists until the day they died.

From 1955 until its closure in 1961, Highlander Folk School was a prolific training ground for the leftist operatives in the Civil Rights Movement who eventually took over the Democratic Party. They trained Rosa Parks before her arrest, as well as Rev. Martin Luther King, Jr., Rev. Ralph Abernathy, Rev. James Bevel, Rev. Andrew Young, Rev. John Lewis, Julian Bond, and many future leaders of the Democratic Party. After training, they were activated and ready to foment revolution not through love as they advertised but through envy, hatred, and inciting and instigating violence.

In their sinister and secretive plans to take over the Democratic Party by subduing the black community, the criminal tactics of the political Left were taken to another sinister level. A close inspection of the history of that era provides a tremendous amount of evidence concluding that Martin Luther King and the activists in the Civil Rights Movement were the front men or "useful idiots" in a successful scheme to secure the black vote by condemning the black community to poverty and slavery through replacing its cultural institutions (education, economy, church, family, and politics) with the atheist/Marxist tenets of state control.

With millions of dormant black votes activated and controlled, leftists would pay the apostate Marxist black preachers in the movement to steer that vote to the Democratic Party, taking control of it and, with it, much of the government of the United States of America.

In an April 4, 2018, article in *USA Today*, James C. Cobb writes that in a Harris Poll in 1968, before his death, Martin Luther King had nearly a 75 percent disapproval rating among all Americans. This is a catastrophic poll. It reflected the people that knew him before the leftists' PR machine exploited his murder to render him a saint.

Maybe they were on to something. The things you will read next may change your mind about the good doctor and where he actually belongs in American history and black history.

This is how it happened.

MARTIN LUTHER KING IS ACTIVATED

Watch out for false prophets. They come to you in sheep's clothing, but inwardly they are ferocious wolves.

By their fruits you will recognize them. Do people pick grapes from thornbushes, or figs from thistles? Likewise, every good tree bears good fruit, but a bad tree bears bad fruit. A good tree cannot bear bad

*fruit, and a bad tree cannot bear good fruit. Every
tree that bears good fruit is cut down and thrown
into the fire.*

Thus, by their fruit you will recognize them.

Matthew 7:15–20

Intentions seem to be the sole criteria recognized by the Left
when measuring any action. Results do not matter. The Civil
Rights Movement is a prime example of this flawed standard. In
every other endeavor, we measure results. As Jesus says, "You will
know them by their fruits." How do you know if a doctor is a good
doctor? Study his patients. How do you know if an architect is a
good architect? Study his buildings. How do you know if a leader
is a good leader? Study his people. Using this metric demanded by
Jesus Christ as a unit of evaluation, Martin Luther King was not
only a terrible leader for black Americans but also a false prophet
for Christianity.

I know some of you are now very emotional, and your heads
are about to explode, but you must set aside emotion and deal
only with the condition of the fruit. If the fruit is rotten, according
to Jesus, the tree must also be rotten. According to the NAACP,
the SCLC, the Urban League, and every socioeconomic statistic
available, the fruit of the black community is rotten to the core.

So why are these people celebrated? Maybe the Civil Rights
Movement and Martin Luther King are celebrated because they
did exactly as instructed. They were not instructed to save the
souls of their people. They were not instructed to teach self-re-
liance, love, forgiveness, or repentance. They were instructed to
teach pride, envy, revenge, and coercion. But most importantly,
they were instructed to organize the black vote and guide it to the

Marxist/leftist candidates on the Democratic Party ticket. They did that very well. Mission accomplished.

Ironically, the betrayal began in the very place that King and his confederates in the SCLC swore to protect. It all started by bastardizing the black community's most cherished institution—the church.

STEP 1: CONTROL THE BLACK CHURCH

King Betrays the Black Church

In September 1961, Martin Luther King concocted a plan to take over the seven-million-member-strong National Baptist Convention, the largest black Christian organization in America. By implementing leftist politics into the black church it seems that he planned to erase the Christian concepts of the church, replacing them with Marxist/Communist politics. Thus, putting the most powerful and autonomous institution in black America under the control of a Civil Rights Movement controlled by counter-culture revolutionaries, atheists, and Communists. This would be the first step in what will eventually be the foreign Marxist takeover of the Democratic Party.

To do so, King had to produce another American oppressed class. The class is an oxymoron called the "Christian victim." Quotes.net records Hellen Keller as saying, "Self-pity is our worst enemy and if we yield to it, we can never do anything wise in this world." She is correct. Obviously, King and his cohorts did not believe it.

Being a "Christian victim" is akin to being a financially poor billionaire or dry and wet. It is self-contradiction. It's impossible. To reject one's wealth is the only way one can be a financially poor billionaire. To reject Jesus Christ and his teachings is the only way one can be a "Christian victim." Christians believe that Jesus Christ is the most powerful being in the universe. He loves me and I am his heir. For this reason, I am not a victim or oppressed nor can I be. The rejection of Jesus and his teachings, leading ultimately to fratricide, calamity, and re-enslavement is where the teaching of Martin Luther King ultimately led black America.

King had the task of convincing black people that all their problems, real and imaginary, were pressed upon them by the all-powerful white man. And that only the government, not Jesus or they themselves, had the power to protect blacks and provide them with all their needs if they begged hard and long enough. Ergo: Jesus Christ had failed them, and they must seek a new God. Now blacks must pray to and serve their new God, the Democratic Party. This ideology was anti-Christian, un-American, and unmanly then and remains so today.

King and other members of the civil rights community, such as the NAACP, the Congress on Racial Equality (CORE), and the Student Nonviolent Coordinating Committee (SNCC), did not believe the admonition in Genesis 4:7: "If you do well, will you not be accepted." Possessing the spirit of Cain, they did not seek to earn acceptance. They were too afraid to take it. They begged a third party, the federal government, to take it for them. The members of the civil rights community were judged by their character—the character of an obsessed stalker.

Most of us now agree that legal segregation based on race is wrong. But I also contend that forced integration based on race is equally wrong. "Force" is "force." Two wrongs never make a right. The fact that King and his cohorts resorted to forcing themselves on white Americans verified what had only been a theory about the black inferiority complex. Furthermore, Christians are never allowed to use any type of extortion to force compliance. Indeed, 1 Corinthians 6:10 says, "extortioners shall not inherit the kingdom of God."

It is illuminating that extortion was not "one" of the tools of these "men of God"; it was their only tool.

King lost faith in the teachings of Christ and turned to the power of the government gun, and Americans are still suffering for it.

King convinced black Americans to break the Tenth Commandment, instructing them to "covet" what their white neighbors possessed. Even rejecting the Christian concept of justice and coveting the Marxist concept of equality and forced assimilation with white Democrats whom King himself had defined as unjust, racist, and lawless. With his need for white acceptance and anger at white rejection, King stoked in the black community envy, hatred, revenge, and unforgiveness. For this reason, Christians are instructed to disregard how they are viewed by men. They should be concerned only about whether God is satisfied with them.

King encouraged blacks to utilize sit-ins, marches, boycotts, and lawsuits to force themselves into the presence of white Americans who did not prefer it. To never offend except for the sake of Christ. These actions were uncharitable and weak. In line more with a demented stalker, not a strong, secure, and sober man of God. Where anywhere in the Bible had we read of any prophet acting this way or instructing others to engage in such actions just to be accepted by men?

King then preached the heresy that this behavior was Christian behavior, reasoning that because blacks believed that whites were superior beings with better schools, restaurants, hotels, water fountains, bathrooms, bus seats, sports teams, movie theaters, and just the general orbit around their whiteness, it was the violation of the civil rights of black people not to be able to force themselves into the presence of white people who did not covet it. Furthermore, the church's traditional focus on ecclesiastical matters like love, forgiveness, virtue, peace, honesty, and the afterlife was not functional for King's new mission. It had to be recreated in his image.

If King had been merely a politician, this would not be near as troublesome. But as a Christian minister his actions are exponentially more visceral. It is the emotion you feel when you hear of a nurse harming a patient, a father raping his daughter, or a priest molesting a little boy. King held a position of ecclesiastical trust. Unlearned people were trained to listen to their preachers and obey because they spoke for God. People who take this trust and use it for personal aggrandizement are the lowest form of human beings. They not only betray the trust that these people have in the man, but they also betray the trust the people have in the institution and God himself. This mistrust can lead to catastrophic consequences. For the black community, it already has.

King introduced the political doctrine of nonviolent resistance as a Christian doctrine, turning young Christians into suicide martyrs for the atheist Communist/Marxist cause here in America. Scores died protesting, marching, and organizing in this successful movement to enslave the black community again to a new, improved, and more malevolent Democratic Party. And like the Mafia, the Democrats would rather see their pawns dead than out.

King's attempted coup against the National Baptist Convention would end with the death of one minister, King's ex-communication from the black church, the birth of an apostate church, and the demotion of the "black church" from a body designed to prepare its parishioners to live forever in the presence of Christ into a lapdog for the Democratic Party. It also began the precipitous demise of the black community from a self-reliant, God-fearing, and family-loving community into a mostly Democratic Party–enslaved divisive mob. King's newly formed apostate sect will help to turn the Democrats into a Marxist cabal. Now the Democrats plan to turn America into the USSR.

The National Baptist Convention was under the control of the Rev. Joseph Jackson of Olivet Baptist Church in Chicago from 1953 to 1982. By all accounts, Rev. Jackson believed in the biblical admonitions in Romans 13 that all laws should be followed. And that Christians should not break the law unless the law forbids them from practicing their religious faith. According to Rev. Jackson, the laws of segregation did not fall under that category.

The right to protest peacefully has always been legal under the Constitution. If the people wanted to protest, it would be during their private time as citizens under the auspices of civilian authority like the NAACP or Urban League, not the ecclesiastical authority of the church. Therefore, Rev. Jackson was not a fan of lawlessness. He did not support the marches and the sit-ins from his congregants, especially for the benign purpose of forcefully integrating with people that hated them. He definitely was not going to side with the Communists and atheists controlling the Civil Rights Movement by sanctioning their ideology from the church. In *Parting the Waters*, Bishop Rev. Jackson was reported to have said, "No matter how non-violent, civil disobedience lays the ground for civil hatred and the desire to destroy." In hindsight, many can say Rev. Jackson was correct.

But Martin Luther King had his marching orders. Thus, he hatched a plan. It started in 1957. It was understood that Rev.

Jackson would not run for re-election. However, Jackson surprised everyone when he stood for re-election and won. According to David Garrow, King was elected vice president. King's plans to take over the National Baptist Convention would have to wait.

In 1961 King had his opportunity. These little-known accounts of the civil war initiated against the black church executed by Dr. Martin Luther King Jr. and its aftermath are supported by two Pulitzer Prize–winning books, *Parting the Waters* by Taylor Branch and *Bearing the Cross* by David Garrow. Ralph David Abernathy's *And the Walls Came Tumbling Down* adds to these accounts. They are further supported by anyone willing to conduct a Google search.

Taylor writes:

> King was scheduled to nominate Gardner Taylor against J.H Jackson at Kansas City. He and his fellow conspirators had spent a year recruiting preachers to come to Kansas City as Taylor's men pledged to uphold the validity of Taylor's election in Philadelphia and they had printed their own "official" credentials and literature, parallel to Jackson's. In an effort to forcibly place Gardener Taylor on the platform with Jackson a struggle broke out between the Taylor and Jackson men. The opposing preachers wrestled, shoved, and punched one another. Rev. A.G. Wright of Detroit a member of the national board and a close personal friend of Rev. Joseph Jackson suffered a fractured skull in the mele. The battle went on for an hour even after Rev. Wright was carried away in an ambulance. A preacher lost

three teeth in one of the many fistfights. It took eight Kansas City Police in riot gear to finally restore order. Rev. Wright died two days after his assault. Rev. Jackson blamed Martin Luther King for Rev. Wright's death.

After all of this plotting mayhem, Rev. Joseph Jackson defeated Rev. Gardener by 2,732 to 1,519. Taylor Branch, on page 505 of *Parting the Waters*, says in the afterword:

> Jackson stripped King of his prestigious title as vice president of the Conventions Sunday School Board. This was the most severe punishment available to him, carrying the sting of a summary court-martial or ex-communication… Absolving Gardner Taylor as the figurehead, he charged that it was Martin Luther King who masterminded the invasion of the convention floor Wednesday, which resulted in the death of a delegate.

Yes. Dr. Martin Luther King Jr., a moral icon of the Left and hero of black America, was excommunicated from the black church for attempting a coup that would have made it part of the Civil Rights Movement and would have also made it part of the atheist Communist Party.

But King didn't give up. He had his orders. Already excommunicated from the church, King convinced his supporters to split from the National Baptist Convention. He then created another competing branch of the black Baptist church—the Progressive Baptist National Convention (PBNC). Stanley Levinson saw to it that his Communist friends in the media either downplayed or

CRIME INC. I

spun the whole incident in King's favor. And even though King could only convince one-tenth of the seven million Baptist members to follow him into ex-communication, he received nearly 100 percent of the media exposure.

The curse of Martin Luther King and the black preacher–led Civil Rights Movement is that it changed the standards and aspirations of most black people. A people who had been mostly concerned with God, family, community, and upward mobility was to be remade. This group of false prophets has trained most black Americans to be more concerned with being equal to or being like white people than being like Jesus. Goodreads.com quotes Fredrick Nietzsche as saying, "Nobody is more inferior than those who insist on being equal." Indeed.

Matthew 6:24 states, "No man can serve two masters; for he will hate one and love the other." Looking at the condition of most black people in America today, which master do you think they serve, and which master do they hate? Most of white America has rejected this insane comparison. But the white leftists scream, "White privilege," putting themselves above all other races. Thus, giving themselves the armor of Godlike power by actually telling inferior-minded blacks, "If you vote for me, I will make you equal to me."

The Civil Rights Movement signaled the beginning of the decline of the black church in America. Too many of them ceased to be ecclesiastical institutions where preparing Christians to forever live in the presence of Jesus Christ was its only purpose and morphed into a slave pen for the Democratic Party.

Instead of concerning itself with pleasing God and the saving of souls, it is more concerned with pleasing the Democratic Party. The black church's primary concerns now are voting, civil rights, LGBTQ+ rights, trans rights, and abortion. Democrats,

37

of course, are elated at this outcome. America, however, is only suffering while black America is devastated.

In a September 30, 2016, piece in the *Washington Post* titled "'The End of Our Journey': A historic black church closes its doors in a changing D.C.," DeNeen L. Brown highlights and inadvertently chronicles the demise of Lincoln Temple United Church of Christ after its transformation from a church designed solely to expound the teachings and worship of Jesus Christ to a church for the Marxist Left:

> One last time, the faithful rose, mounting the steps and flocking into the pews of Lincoln Congregational Temple United Church of Christ, one of Washington's most historically significant African American churches... The death of the renowned church in Shaw—an anchor during decades of segregation, a staging ground for the 1963 March on Washington, and a haven during the 1968 riots—is the latest sign of the capital's changing face as black residents get priced out of this neighborhood and so many others. Black businesses have closed up shop, and black houses of worship have sold their real estate and headed to the suburbs, where most of their congregants live. *A Civil Rights Powerhouse...* In 1963, people attending the March on Washington camped out in the church auditorium...Lincoln Temple designated itself as an "open and affirming" church, welcoming the LGBTQ community... The church held Saturday evening concerts bringing in the

Gay Men's Chorus and the National Symphony. People came. "We had repast downstairs after with wine, cheese, crackers," Cooper said. "I did a little history of the church." But no one returned the next morning for Sunday service.

I wonder why they didn't return. The church is not designed to affirm LGBTQ+; it is designed to call LGBTQ+ and all sinners to repentance and salvation. Christians knew this. This church had lost its mission.

Did you notice that the story did not mention how many souls were saved or how many people were baptized and filled with the Holy Spirit? It did, however, speak about the "open and affirming" LGBTQ environment and the Gay Men's Chorus performing there. This church failed because, like too many churches in America, it became apostate.

Ecclesiastical matters were the primary focus of the Baptist church. In contrast, the progressive Baptist church of Martin Luther King became an apostate institution that relegated the black church to an organizing tool for the progressive Left and Communist takeover of the Democratic Party. The progressive Baptist church preaches Marxism in the form of black liberation theology. It embraces violence, envy, and jealousy in the form of "direct action." And it recently stripped all pretense of Christian orthodoxy by collaborating with openly Marxist and atheist BLM organizations.

For those who say the church can do politics and religion at the same time: Jesus proclaimed, "No man can serve two masters. He will either love one and hate the other." The master of too many black churches is obvious.

STEP 2: CONTROL EDUCATION

Malcolm X opined, "Only a fool would allow his enemy to educate his children." Nevertheless, it was so important for Martin Luther King and the civil rights organizations that black children go to school with and be taught by racist unbelievers that they told Black Americans, The Little Rock 9, Ruby Bridges, Vivian Malone and James Hood, and James Meredith that it was necessary to face death to achieve it.

In a way, America did die. After forcing segregationist compliance in many historical court cases, these racists taught many blacks to hate themselves, their God, and their nation—making far too many blacks slaves to the Democratic Party and the people who control it. Compared to the family-oriented God-fearing people pre-civil rights, black Americans, and now white America today in many ways are unrecognizable and not in a good way.

King and his confederates in the Civil Rights Movement decided to drop an atomic bomb on black people. They decided to remove all black children from the churches and communities that had nurtured, educated, and protected them, turning them over to racist white Democrats who, in words and deeds, left no doubt that they hated and despised black people.

In the Ken Burns documentary on Muhammad Ali, Ali said, "It is a sick mind that fights to be somewhere where he is not wanted." I agree. However, black people were not sick. Their "leadership" was and is still sick. This sickness is contagious.

Controlled by the greatest contributors to the Democratic Party, the Democratic Party–controlled National Education Association (NEA) and the American Federation of Teachers (AFT) witness the sick and demented miseducation and indoctrination these beasts have unleashed upon our children.

On September 23, 2022, on *Tucker Carlson Tonight* on Fox News, Carlson reported on a story published by the Manhattan Institute's Chris Ruffo that outed the largest teachers' union, the NEA. The NEA is one of the largest supporters of the Democratic Party in this country; over 97 percent of its millions of dollars in campaign contributions go to Democrats. It represents three million teachers and is actively advocating the sexualization and grooming of minor children without parental knowledge through its LGBTQ caucus. The LGBTQ caucus of the NEA has produced a website that encourages teachers to talk about sex practices with underage children.

To quote Carlson, "The website specifically shares resources that promise to quote, empower youth and teach them about quote anal sex, bondage, rimming, domination, sadomasochism and something called muffing."

Ruffo revealed that the teachers' union had created badges for public school teachers with a QR code on the back that links them to these resources, including this resource on "queering" sex ed: The idea that traditional sex education is white-male and heterosexual-focused, and that in order to empower LGBTQ+ students, schools have to teach them about the whole range of sex acts, including sadomasochism, bonding, rimming, and then some, is almost unbelievable; the guide is designed to empower youth on fisting, which is defined a putting a fist or whole hand into a person's vagina or bum. This is the teachers' union's official ideology.

Ruffo went on to say that this sick ideology came from the queer academic theories from the colleges and universities of the 1980s and 1990s. Michel Foucault and Gayle Rubin specifically advocated adult-child sexual relationships. AFT president Randi Weingarten is an uncloseted lesbian who calls another woman her wife. Such people in the NEA and ATF are given the task of educating children in the United States of America.

In 1956, a Leftist Supreme Court put the federal government in charge of public education when it decided to cure the inferiority of black children by siding with the leftist NAACP, forcibly integrating them with white children in *Brown v. Board of Education*. The same leftist Supreme Court in 1962 sided with the Leftist New York Civil Liberties Union and ruled prayer in schools illegal in *Engel v. Vitale*. Every attempt to overturn these dangerous opinions with legislation or amendments to the Constitution was blocked by the Marxists in the Democratic Party.

At the time of this debacle, the United States boasted one of the best public education systems in the world. By 1983, twenty-one years later, the United States National Commission on Excellence in Education published "A Nation at Risk." The report said, "If an unfriendly foreign power had attempted to impose on America the mediocre educational performance that exists today, we might have well viewed it as an act of war." A foreign power *had* imposed it: the Communists/Marxists in the USSR through the Democratic Party.

Blacks were told by their "leaders" that they should turn their children over to unbelievers, criminals, and racists for education. Is it any wonder that America's education system is below every other country in the industrialized world and our cities are burning?

This is immoral and, therefore, criminal.

Even though Maryland is the wealthiest and most Democratically controlled state in America, in its predominantly black, poor, and Democrat-controlled city of Baltimore, Democrats in the twenty-first century treat black people with the contempt of 1956.

Baltimore was always a violent city, but in 2016 after the BLM riots commenced, it went to another level with yearly murders between 309 and 348 since then. And while Democrats pressed for LGBTQ+ grooming as the most important issue of our time, *U.S. News & World Report* reported that for the year 2022, the 92-percent-black public school system in Baltimore had a math proficiency score of 17 percent and reading proficiency of 8 percent, even after spending $21,337 per student. On September 23, 2022, public health, education, and medical experts at Johns Hopkins University released a study finding that "the conditions of the school facilities in Baltimore City are clearly the worst in the state."

On September 21, 2021, in a story titled "Baltimore Schools Flunk Nationwide Test," the Maryland Public Policy Institute plainly stated:

> If increasing funding hasn't improved public education in Baltimore City, why aren't Maryland's leaders thinking more creatively about to help these students succeed academically? And if these schools aren't able to meet their student's needs, why are public officials trapping students in these factories of hopelessness, which so consistently fail to prepare young people for the workplace or higher education?

Why should they? The city is a Democrat-controlled plantation. As long as they grow up and vote Democrat and voluntarily remain on the plantation, nothing will change.

On the other hand, in Prince George's County, the richest majority-black county in America, located in Maryland, the wealthiest state in America, crime is so rampant that on September 5, 2022, the *Washington Post* reported black County

Executive Angela D. Alsobrooks announced that a curfew would go into effect for juveniles younger than seventeen "to battle crime after one of the deadliest months in decades. The county had broken records with eight homicides and 355 carjackings through July 2022."

The schools in Prince George's County are not much better than the schools in high-poverty Baltimore. On September 9, 2022, the *Washington Post* reported that less than 25 percent of the students were meeting expectations in math and English/language arts; math tests were lower, with less than 10 percent of students meeting expectations on those tests.

This failure is the legacy of Martin Luther King, the Civil Rights Movement, and the Marxist crime element they helped to establish and maintain in the black community for the Democratic Party.

What is the remedy? Educational freedom through education choice. Get your children out of public education! Vote for candidates who advocate education vouchers, tax credits, scholarships, and charters for private religious schools.

STEP 3: DESTROY THE SOUL

MLK, the Civil Rights Movement, and the Genesis of Abortion

Fratricide is when one murders one's family members or countrymen. Nothing indicates the presence of Satan in a society and the spiritual cancer associated with it than the presence of this sick phenomenon. And Martin Luther King received an award for his work in normalizing fratricide among black Americans.

Margret Sanger, the founder of Planned Parenthood, had a plan to eliminate black people in America. She called it "the

Negro Project." Hiring black preachers to convince black people to murder their children was an integral part of Sanger's plan. It worked to perfection. It is fitting that, as reported by Sangerpaperswordpress.com, the first recipient of the Margaret Sanger award in 1966 was Dr. Martin Luther King, Jr. King's speech from the website is as follows.

> The Negro constitutes half the poor of the nation. Like all poor, Negro and white, they have many unwanted children.
>
> This is a cruel evil they urgently need to control... Some commentators point out that with present birth rates, it will not be long before Negroes are a majority in many of the major cities of the nation. As a consequence, they can be expected to take political control, and many people are apprehensive at this prospect. Negroes do not seek political control by this means... For these reasons, we are natural allies of those who seek to inject any form of planning in our society.

About two weeks after the award ceremony, King wrote a letter to Cass Canfield, chairman of the executive committee of the Planned Parenthood Federation of America's World Population Emergency Campaign:

> Dear Dr. Canfield:
>
> Words are inadequate for me to say how honored I was to be the recipient of the Margaret Sanger Award.

This award will remain among my most cherished possessions.

While I cannot claim to be worthy of such a signal honor, I can assure you that I accept it with deep humility and sincere gratitude. Such a wonderful expression of support is of inestimable value for the continuance of my humble efforts…
I am happy to be the recipient of the Margaret Sanger Award, and I can assure you that this distinct honor will cause me to work even harder for a reign of justice and a rule of love all over our nation.

Planned Parenthood is now responsible for over 63 million abortion murders. Over 20 million of them are black children.

Abortion is the greatest crime in world history. You do not only kill the child. You kill all the children, grandchildren, great-grandchildren, and descendants in perpetuity. You also rob the world of their gifts, crippling all the people they would have blessed.

Sadly, the evidence is unmistakable that Martin Luther King and the Civil Rights Movement collaborated with the political Left to orchestrate the greatest crime in world history.

STEP 4: DESTROY THE FAMILY

MLK, the Civil Rights Movement, and the Destruction of the Black Family

Every social scientist will connect the genesis of the downfall of black America to the destruction of the black family and the absence of the black father. The political Left either ignores the issue completely or deflects, blaming the criminal justice system or hapless Republicans.

However, very few know that Martin Luther King and the Civil Rights Movement were behind the whole thing.

As flawed as it was, the Civil Rights Movement is still hallowed ground in America on both the left and the right. Even America's most conservative scholars, both black and white, either have not researched this problem completely or kowtow to political correctness whenever this era is to be seriously scrutinized. They all give in to the psychological crutch of "effort justification." Believing that the effort put into the Civil Rights Movement, even though it failed, should justify our respect for their effort. It, therefore, should not be scrutinized or questioned without a stern rebuke. To hell with that! I will continue to scrutinize the actions and results of our so-called leaders. If the truth offends, then be offended.

This scrutiny continues with me correcting the history of another atrocious crime committed by Martin Luther King, the Civil Rights Movement, and the political Left. The crime of destroying the family.

While working in the Department of Labor in 1965, Daniel Patrick Moynihan was given the task of helping the Johnson Administration to develop a policy for the war on poverty. While analyzing black poverty, Moynihan noticed a phenomenon. He noticed that starting in 1962, the rate of black male unemployment was going down, while welfare enrollment in the black community was going up. This had never happened before. Nevertheless, the data revealed that it happened again in 1963, 1964, and 1965. This was happening because the Civil Rights Movement's victimization campaign was finally reaping dividends. Before the Civil Rights Movement, black Americans understood that the avenue to success in America passed through education, morality, and hard work. But after 1956, they were told that it came through government handouts. Black women, falling for the lie, were getting on welfare instead of getting married.

Moynihan understood that this problem would eventually destroy the black family and would not fix itself. He understood that the federal government was causing this problem and should be involved in fixing it. Moynihan's 1965 report to the president offered a solution to the problem. He wrote,

> A national effort is required that will give a unity of purpose to the many activities of the federal government in this area, directed to a new kind of national goal: the establishment of a stable Negro family structure... Mitigation of this problem must await those changes in the Negro and American society which will enable the Negro father to play the role required of him... But here is where the true injury has occurred; unless this damage is repaired, all efforts to end discrimination and poverty and injustice will come to little.

Moynihan was correct. And it would soon be revealed to Moynihan that this trend was not a mistake. It was part of a sinister plan orchestrated by the political Left, Martin Luther King, and the Civil Rights Movement.

The fact that Martin Luther King and other members of the civil rights community rejected the plan out of hand during a Ford-funded ministers leadership training program with several hundred civil rights associates in Miami tells the story. David

Garrow in *Bearing the Cross* pages 598–599 writes about the hostile encounter:

> The most heated session featured Daniel Patrick Moynihan, author of a controversial analysis of black family life.
>
> Moynihan spoke in an atmosphere of total hostility, one Ford Foundation observer reported and Moynihan later wrote to Ford President McGeorge Bundy to protest SCLC venture. The session was "the first time I have ever found myself in an atmosphere so suffused with near madness... The leadership of the meeting was in the hands of near demented Black militants who consistently stated one untruth after another (about me, about the United States, about the President, about history, etc., etc.) without a single voice being raised in objection. King, Abernathy and [Andrew] Young sat there throughout, utterly unwilling (at least with me present) to say a word in support of non-violence, integration peaceableness." Ford's observer noted that it was an accomplishment that Moynihan got out alive.

Marx and Engels, the inventor of Communism, believed that the family should be abolished. This is verified by Richard Weikart, in his piece "Marx, Engels and the Abolition of the Family," wrote: "The Utopian Socialists Charles Fourier and Robert Owen had preceded Marx and Engels in their rejection of traditional family relationships and many nineteenth-century leftists followed their cue." Martin Luther King was a twentieth-century leftist. His libertine lifestyle and his rejection of this most human pronouncement of sustainment prove this point.

The primary goal of this cabal during this phase of the movement was family abolition, not preservation. Its members instead lobbied for the "man in the house" clause to be added to the welfare statute demanding that if a man is caught in the house, no government assistance would be provided. Consequently, the rate of black children born out of wedlock skyrocketed from 25 percent in 1966 to almost 70 percent by the end of the 1970s.

King was not interested in protecting the family; he was interested in destroying it. His attention was elsewhere. He had recently met with reporters to announce his demands for the Poor Peoples Campaign. The "family" was never mentioned. Understanding that the entire US budget was $144 billion, King wanted $30 billion. That's the equivalent of someone demanding $2 trillion today. For every American he demanded full employment, a guaranteed annual income, and construction funds for 500,000 units of low-income housing per year. In other words, King wanted Communism.

In the black community, he got it. How does the black community like it?

Government schools, government religion, government economy, 20 million abortions, family were destroyed. All courtesy of Rev. Dr. Martin Luther King, Jr., the Civil Rights Movement, and the political Left.

To the rest of America: Mark well the assault on the black community by these entities. If you love the ghettos of America today, and if you keep voting Democrat, you will love all of America in ten years.

Maintaining the Lie

This history is hidden. I've never met one person, black or white, that knew this history. Obviously, it is known in certain circles. It has been recorded in the books that I cited and is as simple as a Google search but it is buried amongst all the hype in our national discourse. It is not taught in schools. No movies are made about it. Why? Democrats must maintain the lie. Like members of organized crime, Democrats must maintain the lie that they are "men of respect" and "men of honor" when they are really only a cabal of perverts, liars, thieves, and murderers.

What has happened since? With a recorded lifestyle replete with orgies and drunkenness between him and his fellow progressive clergymen, Martin Luther King became more like Rasputin than Jesus. More than a decade of riots, murders, and fire ensued, with black Americans worse off today than before King's arrival.

For those who suffer from willful blindness, falling for the political Left's character assassination of their arch enemy J. Edgar Hoover and the FBI—understand there is too much corroborating evidence, not gathered by the FBI, to confirm that Martin Luther King was not who history says he is.

Ralph Abernathy corroborated King's criminal treatment of women in his book *And the Walls Came Tumbling Down*. Of course, King's apologists attacked Abernathy, calling him a liar and a Judas and accusing him of jealousy. However, none apologized when Dorothy Cotton revealed in an interview with Jason Miller on *The Conversation* on June 24, 2019, that she was King's "other wife." She also verified that King did beat her at the Lorrain Motel the night before his murder after she found out that he slept with Tarlease Mathews (also known as Adjua Naantaanbuu) the same night, and that Kentucky Senator Georgia Powers in the room below just minutes earlier. Before her death, Georgia Powers also confirmed Abernathy's account in her book *I Shared the Dream*.

The first rule of self-love is never to allow yourself to be mistreated or abused by anyone. However, it was King that planted into the black community the lie that there was virtue in black male cowardice by him allowing the mistreatment and abuse of his community by white racists. This black self-hatred inevitably led to the black self-harm of drug addiction, fathers abandoning children, and black-on-black crime.

King's relationships with the Communists Clarence Jones, Hunter Pitts O'Dell, Bayard Rustin, and Stanley Levinson are not disputed.

King's ex-communication from the black church and his starting of his own apostate sect of the Baptist church called the Progressive National Baptist Convention, replete with Marxist political dogma, is not disputed.

King's support of the destruction of black education by supporting the racist *Brown v. Board of Education* opinion that called black children "inferior," thus taking their education from the church and turning it over to racist Democratic state governments is not in dispute.

King's hand in destroying the black economy by participating in sit-ins and boycotts, insinuating that white-owned businesses were better than black-owned businesses, is not in dispute.

King, assisting the Marxist takeover of the Democratic Party by luring unsophisticated black voters to their ranks with the lie that voting would alleviate all of their problems is not disputed.

King's hand in the destruction of the black family by rejecting Moynihan's plan to empower the black father but accepting the plan to have the black father eradicated through the "man in the house" clause in the welfare statute of LBJ's Great Society is not disputed.

And King's accepting the Margaret Sanger Award, introducing abortion into the black community, and collaborating in the greatest crime in history, the murder of 63 million babies, including 20 million black babies, is not disputed.

Nevertheless, if all this evidence doesn't convince you that King's legacy must be re-evaluated, just examine the state of black America. Blacks did everything that King asked of them and are still at the bottom of every socio-economic statistic in America. A tree is known by its fruit. You don't get bad fruit from a good tree. The fruit and the tree will match. The fruit is bad; therefore, the tree is bad. The socio-economic condition of the black community is the fruit. Rev. Dr. Martin Luther King Jr. is the tree.

What should King have done? As a proclaimed ordained minister and theologian, he should have taught his followers to simply follow the teachings of Jesus. He should have taught them to live exemplary Christ-led lives. He should have taught blacks not to be concerned with how they were viewed by white or black men. They should be concerned only with how they are viewed by God.

King should have saved the many atheists, Marxists, and Communists that conspired alongside him with the Gospel of Jesus Christ instead of scheming with them to introduce a new Marxist social order in black America.

He should have taught them to love everyone but not be concerned with whether they are loved in return. He should have taught them that love does not equal abuse. That you must first love yourself. That self-love requires that you never permit anyone's abuse.

He should have taught black people that Christianity is not a religion of non-violence; it is a religion of non-aggression. He should have taught that a man is required to protect and provide for what he loves. There is no virtue in allowing your wife, children, or fellow man to be abused or murdered by evil men. King's nonviolent stance did not change the heart of white racists. It only activated those with guns who would not allow abuse to be inflicted on themselves or others to come to the defense of helpless and cowardly black men. These black men have been pitied or despised. Never respected or feared.

But King was more politician than theologian.

King was assassinated and made a martyr. His martyrdom placed upon King and his flawed ideology a Christ-like legitimacy that has galvanized his authority in every denomination of the black church and politics. After which, every radical black preacher, politician, and civic organizer joined the only American political party wicked enough to accept its ideas: the Democratic Party.

FOREIGN INFLUENCE IN MILITANT BLACK ORGANIZATIONS

These Marxist/Communist influences cared nothing for violent versus non-violent ideology in the Civil Rights Movement. They only cared whether any black organization intended to overthrow the Christian democratic social order of the United States of America and recruit the black vote to assist in their eventual takeover of the Democratic Party. Like organized crime, these Marxists required an area where their evil would not only be tolerated but also protected. So like Lenin, Castro, and Mao, the anti-heroes and corrupting influences of the black community have been redefined as role models.

Even the radical leftist, Marxist, anti-police organization the Black Panthers, which has been memorialized as protector and benefactor of the black community, was actually nothing more than a group of violent, anti-American doped-out thugs. In order to buy guns, the Panthers sold copies of Mao Zedong's "Little Red Book" on the streets of America. Praising the police state of the USSR and North Korea, they had a name for their political philosophy: "Panther Stalinism."

On the Workers' Liberty website, Dan Katz refers to two books about the Black Panthers. One by Bobby Seale, *Seize the Time*, and *A Taste of Power* by Elaine Brown. In *A Taste of Power*, Brown provides a vivid description of how Panther chairman Bobby Seale had her taken to a basement and whipped because of a disagreement about the Panther newspaper. She later witnessed Hughey Newton driving Bobby Seal out of the Panthers by having his 6'8" bodyguard so severely beat his friend and co-founder with a bullwhip, applying twenty-five lashes, that he needed extensive medical treatment for his injuries. Afterward, it was reported that Seale went into hiding for nearly a year.

On March 23, 2006, from the website workersliberty.org, from a piece called "Cult of the Gun," AWL wrote, "In essence, the Panthers were a proud, dramatic, armed, semi-suicidal defiance of the brutal power which crushed Black People... The Panther regime Brown describes owes more to the structure of a gang than that of a political party."

Even though the Panthers claimed to be vehemently anti-drug, Panther member Flores Forbes, interviewed for the *American Gangster* episode about Oakland heroin kingpin Felix Mitchell, said that Panther chairman Huey Newton made a deal with the notorious drug kingpin Mitchell to sell his heroin on the streets of Oakland if Mitchell paid the Panthers a "street tax." According to *Forbes*, the much-glamorized Black Panther Party was nothing more than an organized crime syndicate used by the political Left to destabilize the United States of America. Their refined history of swashbuckling freedom fighters for black America is still utilized by the Left to lead generation after generation of young people down the false dead-end path of protest, violence, poverty, prison, and death.

Through movies like *Panther, Judas and the Black Messiah, The Trial of the Chicago Eight,* and *Night Catches Us,* like a cerebral vortex, the political Left, through the power of Hollywood, continues to hold black Americans in a time warp of 1960s protest. This is the neo-plantation at work. While white liberals live in penthouses in California and Manhattan, they need their slaves in the fields doing the hard labor.

Even the famed and gallant Huey Newton succumbed. On August 22, 1989, he was murdered by Tyrone Robinson. Reports were that Newton had become addicted to drugs and had stolen drugs from the Black Guerrilla Family. During a drug deal with Newton, Robinson reportedly shot him three times. Robinson said his motive was to advance in the Black Guerrilla Family, another Marxist-Leninist prison gang, in order to get a crack franchise.

In the Mafia, there exists a hierarchy. This hierarchy is foreign and un-American. The bosses at the top live like kings while the pawns at the bottom do all the work, take all the beatings, go to prison, and die.

But, more sadly, this hierarchy has established a culture where the Panthers' immoral, traitorous, and dysfunctional leadership is lionized and worshipped among the young and the poor, guaranteeing an unlimited reservoir for which to draw willing recruits.

Movies are made about Mafia Dons Carlo Gambino, Lucky Luciano, Myer Lansky, and Bugsy Seigel, depicting them as heroes. Hollywood even created fake Mafia Dons like Vito Corleone,

Michael Corleone, and Tony Soprano to brainwash the young into the arbitrary world of organized crime. Likewise, the political Left exploits the tragedies of Martin Luther King, Huey Newton, W. E. B. Dubois, Black Lives Matter, and the Black Panthers to brainwash black American youth into a suicidal mindset and white Americans into a continual state of guilt and condemnation of other whites.

They trap the black American poor and youth into a perpetual state of protest and mental slavery for the benefit of the political Left and the Democratic Party.

The political Left in the Democratic Party has adopted this foreign and criminal hierarchy from the USSR. It works for them. It doesn't matter how many of our children die as their pawns. They will not stop until we make them.

When you remember the murders of Michael Schwerner, Andrew Goodman, and James Chaney, the four little black girls killed in Alabama, the Orangeburg Massacre, Medgar Evers, the Little Rock Nine, Ruby Bridges, the Edmund Pettis Bridge, and the Freedom Riders, you may ask why Southern black people choose to forcibly integrate with people who would do such horrible things. The answer is they didn't. Instead of being a grassroots movement started and sustained by the local people, the Civil Rights Movement was an Astroturf movement tailor-made for TV.

The vast majority of Southern blacks did not finance the Civil Rights Movement, protest in it, or agree with its agenda. Most of the participants were recruited and bused in from the North. They sought out court cases along with stupid belligerent law enforcement officials to antagonize. They instigated violence and welcomed the murder of innocents to gain publicity and public outrage.

These veterans of the "movement" loaned their faux moral absoluteness to every anti-American, anti-white, anti-religion, anti-Protestant, anti-family, and immoral organization in America. Thus, like all American organized crime syndicates, there is no doubt that the genesis of today's Democratic Party was conceived, financed, and organized with foreign ideas by a foreign nation. But this foreign nation was our mortal enemy and wanted our blood. It still does. It was called the USSR then. It's called the Democratic Party now.

The black community in America needs to understand that it can kneel to the false god of black holidays (Juneteenth and MLK day), march, and protest every day. Blacks can tear down all of the Confederate statutes, rewrite American history, receive reparations, celebrate Black History Month, force an apology from every white American, fund every historically black college or university (HBCU), abort every one of their children, and allow the sexual grooming of all of the children they decide not to murder by the Democratic Party—until they decide to reject the ideology of the Democratic Party and the political Left, and start to live again by traditional values and natural law, America can never know its true glory. And as a people, they will remain at the bottom of every socio-economic statistic in the industrialized world.

CHAPTER 2

♣

I WILL BURN IN HELL FOR YOU

This is the man [Tony Soprano]
that I'm going to hell for.
Christopher Moltisanti, *The Sopranos*

In Cormac McCarthy's great book *No Country for Old Men*, because of the illegal drug trade, the protagonist, Sheriff Bell, witnesses an extraordinary amount of violence in his once peaceful county. Unwilling to do what was necessary in response to this violence, Bell concluded that he must resign his office. In explaining why he had made this fateful decision, he said: "I can't say that it's even what I'm willin' to do. I think it is more like what you are willin' to become. And I think a man would have to put his soul at hazard."

Sheriff Bell was not willing to burn in hell for a job. The day I left the Democratic Party forever, I made a similar decision. For my entire life, like most black Americans, my family and I were uninformed members of the Democratic Party. But it was in 1992, when the Democratic Party added the following to its platform, that I decided, unlike many others, that I would not burn in hell for it: "Democrats stand behind the right of every woman to choose, consistent with *Roe v. Wade,* regardless of ability to pay, and support a national law to protect that right."

I was finished with the Democrats. It didn't take any goading, pressure, or persuading. Unlike Sheriff Bell, it wasn't just what I was unwilling to become that made me leave; it was what I was unwilling to do: I would not go to hell for them! To remain a Democrat, through abortion, I would have to become a mass murderer. By accepting LGTQ+ indoctrination, I would have to reject my Lord and Savior, Jesus Christ. I would have to choose man over God.

The first Commandment is plain "Thou shalt have no other gods above me." I wouldn't turn against my God or go to hell for anyone; double that when considering a political party. It was easy for me. I was amazed to find that it wasn't easy for others. I naïvely believed that if Christian men and women received the truth, they would respond as I had. I believed that they would choose God over the Democratic Party. I was in for the shock of my life. I was and am still amazed that people who profess Christianity have volunteered to go to hell for the Democratic Party.

In their satanic connection to organized crime, it seems Democrats have incorporated a blood oath from their followers: The Party is everything. You are nothing. "You will go to hell for us!" As with the Mafia, Democrats have convinced their followers to sacrifice their children, spouses, families, economies, religion, education, and freedom to them.

To demonstrate how you would burn if you betrayed the family, the ritual incorporating individuals into the Mafia involved burning a picture of a saint. The Mafia oath stated: "As burns this saint so will burn my soul. I enter alive, and I will have to get out dead." Most Democratic Party members have psychologically and voluntarily incorporated this blood oath. Employing the rules of a death cult, black Americans who leave the Democratic Party risk not just ostracization and ridicule but also physical harm. Therefore, the Democrats have a license to do anything to their followers without fear of repercussion or reprisal, and they have. As economist Thomas Sowell opined on Brainyquote.com, "It is hard to imagine a more stupid or more dangerous way of making decisions than by putting those decisions in the hands of people who pay no price for being wrong."

There has been a chilling effect on the political Left taking over the Democratic Party. The Left has purged most of the true Christians from the ranks of its leadership, keeping and recruiting most of the phony or stupid Christians en masse. Policies that Democrats once denied for fear of a Christian backlash are now proudly highlighted: same-sex marriage, transgender indoctrination, atheism, sexual grooming of children, legalized drugs, and unrestricted abortion until birth—all immoral, all destructive, all antisocial, all anti-Christian. These atrocities are not just protected as rights but encouraged as righteous behavior. Furthermore, in a twisted ironic fulfillment of prophecy, Democrats are now convincing the population that this devastatingly destructive behavior is righteous. But like organized crime families, a sick loyalty exists within the party. The Democratic leadership exploits this loyalty advantage to the detriment of the nation.

Segments of the population are routinely tested. They have shamelessly proven under the most intense scrutiny that they will not only burn in hell for the Democratic Party; they will educate their children to do the same. They escort them to their schools for indoctrination. They escort them to their welfare offices for victimization. They escort them to the courts for incarceration. All while, like the slaves, giving the Democratic Party permission and power to oppress them and their offspring forever.

The Independent reported on July 16, 1994: "When Stalin died, on March 5, 1953, prisoners in countless labor camps of the Gulag wept." Sadly, like the prisoners in the Gulags, the odds of these people changing are slim. The Democratic Party and the Communists have been successful at replicating the loyalty of organized crime among its members. Organized crime and inner-city gangs have millions of members dead in graveyards or alive in prison, who, like the prisoners in the Communist Gulags, remain loyal to the Democrats who arrested, tried, and convicted them. Moreover, not-yet-dead or not-yet-incarcerated members readily confess that they live in the hell of Democrat-controlled inner cities. Worse, like their forefathers indoctrinated in the Democratic Party plantation culture, these modern-day slaves instruct their children to obey the commands of their Democratic masters, even if it means sacrificing their souls to hell.

I am rational. Information and facts can change my mind. Most of the people on the political Left are highly emotional. This emotion has caused them to place not only their physical bodies but also their immortal souls in jeopardy. Three areas exist where one should never allow emotion to overcome rational thought: money, justice, and politics. The political Left and most Democrats miserably fail at all three.

In his book *The Great Divorce*, C. S. Lewis wrote that Hell is a choice:

> There are only two kinds of people in the end:
>
> Those who say to God, "Thy will be done," and those to whom God says, in the end, "Thy will be done." All that are in Hell, choose it. Without that self-choice, there could be no Hell. No soul that seriously and constantly desires joy will ever miss it. Those who seek find. Those who knock, it is opened.

These Democrats are choosing hell on earth for millions of people. The good news is: They can also un-choose it. They can choose to educate their children in a world of private religious schools, connecting them with God. Their young men will be strong, wise, employable, law-abiding, and respected; their young women, chaste, virtuous, and industrious. They could choose safety over chaos, love over hate, family over dysfunction, children over infanticide, and life over murder. Or they can continually choose the Democrats.

Deuteronomy 30:19 says, "I call heaven and earth to record this day against you, that I have set before you life and death, blessing and cursing: therefore choose life, that both thou and thy seed may live."

The Democratic Party is a death cult. Wherever it rules, whether in San Francisco, Los Angeles, Memphis, Detroit, Philadelphia, Baltimore, or Washington, D.C., hell on earth and early death are present. Do not go to hell for them. Do not escort your children to hell for them. Send them to hell, instead.

CHAPTER 3

♣

THE HUMILIATION OF BLACK PEOPLE

*In my city, we would keep the [drug] traffic
in the dark people; the coloreds. They're
animals anyway, so let them lose their souls.*
"Don" Joseph Zaluchi, *The Godfather*

I n the movie *The Color Purple*, Sofia was a large, proud black
woman who did not allow herself to be disrespected or abused.
In one scene, after answering "Hell no" to the question of
whether she would serve as the maid to the mayor's wife, the
mayor slapped her. Sofia responded with a right hook that landed
the mayor on his back. Understanding that she had broken one
of the seminal codes of the South, and understanding that she
could not rely on her two black male companions for protection,
Sofia—not wanting her children to witness what would happen
to her—screamed for the two cowardly black men to "get my children out of here!"

As an angry mob surrounded her, she spotted the sheriff and screamed to him for help. He instead hit her with the butt of his pistol, rendering her unconscious. To compound her indignity, when she fell, the wind blew up her dress, exposing her underwear for public view.

In the TV miniseries *Roots*, the African slave Kunta Kinte would not answer to his English name Toby. After being recaptured during an unsuccessful escape attempt, the white overseer promised Toby that he would answer to his name. In the presence of all the slaves at the plantation, Kunta was tied to the whipping post by traitorous fellow Black sellout slaves. After dozens of lashes from a traitor slave, Kunta still would not say his name was Toby. Finally, inches from death, Kunta was asked once again by the overseer to say his name. Finally, to save his life, he whispered, "My name is Toby." Kunta's humiliation and demoralization were complete.

This type of indignity and humiliation toward the black community is necessary for organized crime and the Democratic Party to survive. Democrats needed the humiliated and demoralized black population before the Civil War for labor, sex, and social supremacy. They humiliate and demoralize blacks today for votes and monetization through government programs, contracts, and unions. The mental castration of the black man, the exploitation of black women, and the traumatizing of black children are their specialties. From watching the rape of their wives and daughters to the murder and selling of their sons, most black men were taught by their Democrat masters to act as cowards among barbarians.

In the wealthiest country in the world, with every resource known to man, why is the public education system going backward? Why are there ghettos? Why is the black community anchored at the bottom of every socio-economic statistic in America? Because there are people that benefit from it.

Humiliation is an instrument of control wielded by organized crime and the Democratic Party. Why humiliation? As George Orwell wrote in *1984*,

> Obedience is not enough. Unless he is suffering, how can you be sure that he is obeying your will and not his own? Power is in inflicting pain and humiliation. Power is in tearing human minds to pieces and putting them together again in new shapes of your own choosing.

As organized crime coddles every opportunity to humiliate its victims, Democrats do the same. It is the ultimate power move. They have always humiliated black Americans. Rape, castration, whippings, selling family members, house negro leadership, and begging were all humiliations designed for demoralization and control during slavery and today.

Democrats still choose ignoramuses like Rev. Al Sharpton, Congressman Jim Clyburn, and Senator Raphael Warnock as spokesmen. They still castrate black men through unemployment, gun confiscation, miseducation, and incarceration. They still rape their women with a government husband and free abortion. They still abuse their children by selling them on the auction block of sexual grooming, fatherlessness, LGBTQ indoctrination, drugs, and violence. Democrats still choose black heroes from the cesspool and cowards of the community. Drug dealers, apostate preachers, rappers, hip-hop "artists," sellout politicians, and ignorant athletes are the chosen heroes among black Americans.

Every natural disaster is another opportunity for humiliation. Whether it is waiting in line for water, food, transportation, safety, or housing, Democrats will never miss an opportunity to humiliate the black population that they control.

Like pimps with prostitutes, loan sharks with borrowers, pushers with junkies, gamblers with bookies, coyotes with illegal immigrants, extortioners with the extorted, and Democrats with black Americans, humiliation is a tactic of control and power resulting in demoralization. And a demoralized person cannot participate in his own liberation.

Understand that slavery is a choice, and no one can be a slave without his or her own permission. When it comes to convincing the weak and fearful of surrendering the rights that secure their freedoms, Democratic conmen are masters. The way a charlatan shrewdly convinced the naive and stupid Jack to surrender the essential family cow for magic beans, Democrats have convinced blacks to relinquish their essential rights to educate their children and to practice their religion. Most importantly, blacks have been convinced to surrender their unalienable right to self-defense. The only animal that can be convinced to roam this earth after voluntarily conceding its right and ability to self-defend is a pet.

I contend that there is another sinister incentive for the trade of liberty for security: revenge. Revenge for wrongs done is one of the primary incentives given by weak people who follow Communists and join organized crime. Lenin and the Communists murdered Russia's royal family and confiscated the wealth of the bourgeoisie. Mao, Castro, and Ho duplicated these tactics. Marxists here in America have promised the same. They have promised to confiscate wealth, award reparations, impose reverse racism, censor disagreeable speech, and violently punish or imprison those who do not fall in line. Aldous Huxley once stated,

> The surest way to work up a crusade in favor of some good cause is to promise people they will have a chance of maltreating someone.
>
> To be able to destroy with good conscience, to be able to behave badly and call your bad behavior "righteous indignation"—this is the height of psychological luxury, the most delicious of moral treats.

From lessons derived from the old plantation system, Democrats understand that there is power in dominating a perpetually uneducated, poor, and fearful populace. If these conditions do not naturally occur, they must be manufactured artificially. Unnaturally contriving the environment that manufactures these conditions is the primary reason the partnership between the political Left, Democrats, and organized crime exists.

All organized crime syndicates understand that to function without blowback from the police or middle-class and upper-class communities, territories must be set aside among marginalized and desperate people outside these communities. In most other countries, these territories were determined by class. Poor people do not carry much political capital; thus, the sultry dealing of the underworld usually prospered in their midst.

But here in America, because of a sinister hatred of black Americans by the Mafia and the Democratic Party leadership, whether it be affluent, majority-black Prince George's County in Maryland or the poverty-stricken ghettos of Memphis, Tennessee,

most other Democratic Party of their criminal activity is reserved
for the confines of their perpetual doormat, the black community.

No organizations in the history of the world, past or present, have been responsible for more hatred toward black people
or more deaths of black people than the Democratic Party and
organized crime, but I repeat myself.

For five Senate campaigns from 1920 to 1944, Democratic
Senator Cotton "Ed" Smith won on the campaign slogan "Keep
the Niggers down and the price of cotton up." And while he
supervises a cultural genocide in the black community, President
Joe Biden said as a candidate that if a black person does not vote
for him, "You ain't black."

When it became unfashionable to outright cheat and kill
black Americans while calling them "niggers," the political Left
quickly pivoted from the hatred of oppression to the condescending lie of paternalism. After discovering that Stockholm
syndrome and cognitive dissonance fueled an almost universal
loyalty among black voters to white Democrats, these racists
began to champion more racism as the remedy to supposedly
ending the very racism that they advocated. When Democrats
could no longer use race to exploit the ignorant black laborer
physically, they used it to exploit him mentally and spiritually.

The great C. S. Lewis wrote:

> Of all the tyrannies, a tyranny sincerely exer-
> cised for the good of its victims may be the most
> oppressive. It would be better to live under rob-
> ber barons than under omnipotent moral busy-
> bodies. The robber baron's cruelty may some-
> times sleep, his cupidity may at some point be
> satiated, but those who torment us for our own

good will torment us without end for they do so
with the approval of their own conscience.

Consider this, to make it harder to cheat in elections,
Republicans requested voter ID. Democrats lobbied against this
measure, citing the lie that black people were incapable of attain-
ing photo identification. This idea is condescending and racist.
Black people are not stupid. The real reason: Democrats now
know that every black vote is usually a Democrat vote. Their goal
then is to exploit the Stockholm syndrome existing in the black
community, enticing many through bribery with "street money"
and "souls to the polls" to vote early and often. Voter ID would
destroy this chicanery. Eliminating voter identification allows
Democrats innumerable ways to cheat.

Democrats advocate the expansion and government funding
of abortion by saying it will help poor black women. The real reason: Democrats profit from each abortion, with the added benefit
of fulfilling their need for murder and bloodlust.

Democrats say they advocate more welfare because it helps
poor black people. The real reason: Democrats use welfare as a
tool of control—buying votes—inducing government dependence and ensuring their electoral dominance.

Democrats advocate more government money in the ghetto
neo-plantation education system claiming that it will help black
children. The real reason: The teachers' unions contribute tens of
millions of dollars to the Democratic Party. In return, the unions
demand higher salaries and education slavery for America's children from Democratic politicians. Democrats maintain this
monopoly by blocking educational freedom and choice through
vouchers, charter schools, tax credits, grants, and scholarships.

Democrats and unions prefer an uneducated electorate to an educated one. They are both looking for slaves. As Frederick Douglass said, "An educated man is unfit to be a slave."

When modernizing and investing in decrepit black neighborhoods, Democrats halt the progress by calling it gentrification. The real reason: Democrats do not want middle-class Americans moving into the black ghettos they created. Upper-middle-class voters are much less reliable than the ghetto-minded inner-city blacks, of whom Democrats have near-absolute control.

When America decides to stop the violence and crime in black communities, Democrats charge racial profiling. The real reason: Violence is a tool of control for Democrats, and crime is their primary source of income. Therefore, Democrats have no interest in ending violence in these communities. If anything, they will choose to increase it.

Whenever gangs, drugs, and murder litter the streets, Democrats say we must make all guns illegal. The real reason: Democrats must exploit and oppress black people. They know you cannot oppress an armed population.

When it is proven that abstinence, family, and religion are the remedy to every problem facing America, Democrats justify their assault on these institutions by citing the lie that black women do not desire marriage, black children desire sex education, and because of slavery, black men cannot be expected to be responsible, loving, and caring fathers and husbands. The real reason: Democrats know that if the family structure exists, they will never be allowed to sexualize and exploit black children. Therefore, it was a necessity to destroy this structure.

In other words, before the Civil Rights Movement, Democrats were honest: Racism, hatred, and the continuation of the social order was the Democrats' reason for oppressing black Americans. Now, Democrats exploit black pain for white Democrat political gain. The fact that black Americans will vote for white or black Democrats unconditionally has given black Americans the exact same value as a slave willing to work without pay. This type of blind commitment is rare. Good people will appreciate this loyalty, reward it, and hold you in high esteem. However, evil people, the ones that make up the political Left and the Democratic Party, will hold you in utter contempt.

They will exploit you, mistreat you, and in the end, hate you. Every ghetto, failing school, drug corner, and prostitute house derives from this evil—the evil of exploitation and the self-hatred that allows it. For until you learn to love yourself and understand your value, no one else will, and there will always be a pack of howling hyenas willing and ready to tear at your flesh and shed your blood for the pure enjoyment of it.

To those who are compelled to doubt me because they cannot believe that this type of evil is intentionally orchestrated: I can only refer you to history and the fact that every tyrant, including the Democratic Party, depended on the child-like beliefs of the willfully blind populace as security against the truth. Clear-eyed men and women know that some men are beasts.

Throughout my life, I have confronted and encountered these beasts. They gravitate to one another. They organize and run in packs for protection and for impact. Like the Mafia, Crips, and Bloods, the most political beasts run with the Democratic Party.

Like clockwork, every four years, when the evidence of their failure is again splattered across every news headline, they deflect responsibility while admitting that they "still have work to do." And for some reason, their long-suffering constituents always believe the lie. It is my hope that one day they will heed the advice of George Washington when he wrote in a letter to Fielding Lewis on June 28, 1781,

> A Man may err, and he may err twice but when those who possess more than a common share of abilities persevere in a regular course of destructive policy, one is more apt to suspect their hearts than their heads.

This partnership between organized crime and the Democratic Party began after the transatlantic slave trade constitutionally ended in 1808. Outlawed slave traders continued their activities, delivering Africans to the Democrat-controlled South until the end of the Civil War. After the Civil War, criminal organizations like the Ku Klux Klan controlled the black community for the Democratic Party in the South, while the Mafia controlled the black community for the Democratic Party in the North. Nothing has changed except for color in most instances. Bribery, intimidation, fraud, and murder are committed all to maintain power for the political Left, the Democrats, and money for organized crime. And it works.

Organized crime has a perpetual customer base in the black community, and the Democrats have a perpetual throng of victims. Intellctualtakeout.org featured a 1984 interview by Russian dissident Yuri Bezmenov, a KGB informant and disinformation expert who defected to Canada, explained how the Communists in the Soviet Union gained and maintained control:

> A person who is demoralized is unable to assess true information. The facts tell them nothing, even if I showered them with information, with authentic proof, with documents and pictures...

he will refuse to believe it. Once people's morals have been debased...education becomes indoctrination; entertainment becomes hypnotism; criminals become "leaders," and lies become truth.

In these black ghettos, the most successful criminal enterprise, the Democratic Party, has retained absolute control for over two hundred years through open-air drug markets, gangs, gun control, and general dystopia. Yuri Bezmenov was correct; the criminals are the leaders. Because organized crime is instrumental in demoralizing the people, the people cannot hear the truth. Therefore, the Democratic Party constantly wins 90 percent of the black vote, allowing organized, crime-free reign.

The same conditions of crime, drug abuse, and poverty—the reasons for the very existence of the Democrats—are caused by Democratic Party policies that encourage organized crime. Defunding the police, zero bail, lenient prosecutors, and woke Democratic big-city mayors are just a few ways the Democrats and organized crime exploit black people.

Because of their hatred for black people, the Mafia always initiates its drug trade, number rackets, and prostitution dens in Harlem, Watts, Liberty City, and every black ghetto with the help of black traitors. Democrats do the same.

They both need to exploit the black community in order to survive. Like bloodsuckers, they both exploit it. However, identical to the transatlantic African slave trade, organized crime and the leftists in the Democratic Party must have traitors within the black community to have a fleeting chance of success. There were traitors in Africa who sold their people, and there are black traitors here who do the same.

Organized crime recruited and cultivated notorious black drug kingpins like "Highway" Rick Ross in Los Angeles, Rayful Edmond in Washington, DC, Frank Lucas and Nicky Barnes in Harlem, Felix Mitchell in Oakland, and Coleman Young in Detroit.

Organized crime controls the murderous, misogynistic, and contemptuous hip-hop industry by managing and bankrolling poisonous recording companies like Death Row, Murder, Inc., Bad Boy, Ruff Ryder, and Def Jam. This exact template is recycled politically by Democrats in every inner-city community, except the traitors now are most black preachers, black civic organizations, and black politicians.

The political Left's exploitation of Jackie Smith in Memphis, Tennessee, is a visual representation of what it and the Democratic Party expect from black Americans and the inevitable result of their exploitation. Ms. Smith was the last resident of the place where Martin Luther King Jr. was assassinated, the Lorraine Motel in Memphis.

She worked there as a maid for eleven years earning ten dollars per day plus room and board. In 1988, the Lorraine Motel was sold to a consortium of investors with the intent of turning it into a civil rights museum. After the purchase, all residents were given a certain amount of time to find another place to live or face eviction. Ms. Smith refused to leave and swore she would resist at every step. The standoff became a local news sensation.

Ms. Smith was offered other better housing and a job by the city. She refused. And true to her word, the morning of her court-ordered eviction, four female police officers picked her up by each of her limbs and carried her down a flight of stairs. Jackie Smith kicked, screamed, and flailed about, making the officers' job

. as difficult as possible. It was one of the saddest things I had ever seen in my life. I will never forget it.

After moving Ms. Smith and all her possessions to the curb and threatening her with jail if she ever stepped foot on the premises again, Ms. Smith made a vow to never leave that spot and to protest until her eviction is overturned.

Thirty-four years later, Jackie Smith is still there at the corner of Butler and Mulberry Streets in Memphis, across from the Lorraine Motel. She has broken the record of anti-pedophile protestor John Wojnowski with over 12,000 days of protest. Wojnowski only had 7,300.

As the world continued to spin, something kept Jackie Smith trapped in a 1988 time loop. She never married. Never had children. She never owned a home. And she never was allowed back into the Lorraine Motel. And there is the rub. The political Left encourages people to protest for what they already have or for something that is impossible to attain.

They demand that we protest for "freedom or peace," things we already possess and only need to activate, or for "equality or an end to racism," something that is unattainable. The inevitable disappointment that arrives from protesting for something that is unattainable causes envy, hatred, and pride. Some can say that Ms. Smith is soaked in it.

However, while comfortable at home, her friends on the Left commend her discipline and stick-to-itiveness and display her as a shining example of what all black Americans should be: poor, uneducated, dependent, and exploited.

CHAPTER 4

GROOMING CHILDREN
AS RECRUITS

*I'm Moe Green. I was making my bones
when you were dating cheerleaders.*
Moe Green, *The Godfather*

On October 6, 1963, President John F. Kennedy said: "A nation reveals itself not only by the men it produces but also by the men it honors, the men it remembers." What happens when a nation celebrates stalkers, beggars, victims, and criminals? The nation becomes a dystopia. It becomes suicidal. In *The Republic*, Plato wrote that the well-nurtured child is one,

> who would see most clearly whatever was amiss
> in the ill-made works of man or ill-grown works
> of nature, and with a just distaste would blame
> and hate the ugly even from his earliest years and
> give delighted praise to beauty, receiving it into

his soul and being nourished by it, so he becomes
a man of gentle heart.

Presently, too many children cannot see what is amiss in the
"ill-made" works of man or the "ill-grown" works of nature. The
political Left and the Democrats are grooming them to reject
charm, grace, and elegance and to celebrate the vile, the grotesque,
and the deformed. Too many children lack "gentle hearts" and are
corrupted not long past infancy. Our overcrowded prisons and
the public mass suicide of our young testify to this fact.

With all the evidence to the contrary, evil people still consistently attempt to harm and corrupt other people's children and
believe that they will not be harmed in return. Of all the games
one can play, at one time, this is the most dangerous. Most parents would kill to protect their children. A mother lion locked in
a cage with her cubs isn't there for her protection; she's there for
yours. But Democrats have found a way to use the power of government to punish parents who attempt to protect their children
from the Left by having the US Department of Justice declare
them terrorists.

On March 4, 2022, Texas Attorney General Ken Paxton
issued a press release. He reported on a letter he wrote to US
Attorney General Merrick Garland. In the letter he asked,

> why the National School Board Association
> asked The Department of Justice to invoke the
> Patriot Act to stifle parents from speaking up
> at school board meetings challenging their chil-
> dren's indoctrination through liberal texts and
> racially charged, anti-white lessons, as well as
> the continuation of school mask mandate and
> remote learning.

That's right. If you do not allow the government education system to sexually groom and liberally indoctrinate your children, the Leftist-, Marxist-, Communist-, and Democrat-controlled government plans to mark you a terrorist. Like the Mafia and street gangs, the Democrats need child soldiers and are willing to intimidate and harm parents to achieve it. There is no excuse for parents who allow this tyranny and child abuse while supporting the Democratic Party that applies it.

To highlight this point, on March 2, 2023, in a story titled "Education bill died, but trans debate stirs," Karen Elwood of the *Washington Post* reported about two bills blocked by Democrats that would have made it harder for Democrats in the state of Virginia to use public education to groom children. The *Post* said:

> A week before the session ended, Senate democrats killed two bills, one that would have required students in public schools to compete in sports under the gender they were assigned at birth, and another that would have required school administrators to notify parents if a child identified as a gender different from their biological sex. Both bills survived a floor vote in the Republican-controlled House, marking the first time that measures targeting transgender youths have been passed by a Virginia legislative chamber.

Where do monsters and victims come from? They both are made by beasts. Mafia crime boss Joseph Bonanno said, "Mafia is a process, not a thing. Mafia is a form of clan—cooperation to which its individual members pledge lifelong loyalty."

All organized crime organizations groom children without the knowledge of their parents at the earliest opportunity.

We must turn this development back at all costs. But Democrats are on the attack. If you do not allow the Democrats to groom your children, you are labeled a homophobe or full of hate. If you do not allow them to literally castrate your son, they say you are not allowing "gender-affirming care."

In America, we pride ourselves on our freedom. Even the freedom to destroy ourselves. We are now grappling with a question. Does an adult, hellbent on self-destruction, have the right to teach children to destroy themselves? Do LGBTQ men and women have the right to groom children of parents who find the lifestyle abhorrent to not just accept the lifestyle but engage in the lifestyle?

Unless one has a mental disability, all behavior is learned and controllable. The Left teaches that this is not true. LGBTQ+ doctrine teaches children that they should be led by their passions and should despise people who are not. More than anything, they teach them the suicidal concept that how they see themselves sexually and how freely they express it is the most important aspect of their lives. This obsession with sex by the Democratic Party leadership and how it intends to use your children for their pleasure should be the concern of every parent. But some parents are so enamored by the perverts in the Democratic Party they have already gladly sacrificed themselves and their children.

To highlight this point, former Secretary of Education Betsy DeVos retweeted a tweet from the Democratic Left's most prolific child-grooming organization, the National Education Association (NEA). The tweet read: "Educators love their students and know better than anyone what they need to learn and to thrive." Notice the NEA did not say "parents" know better; it said "educators" know better. The NEA and, by extension, the Democratic Party, a criminal corporation, have taken possession of the country's children and relinquished parents from all authority. They now decide what is best for your children. In their opinion, it is best that your children obey them, not you.

To maintain an adequate number of children to groom and recruit into their nefarious activities, the political Left, Democrats, and organized crime know that few children could be allowed a Christian education. A Christian education would teach children to obey the law, obtain legal employment, abstain from premarital sex, abstain from illegal drugs, never abort a child, never engage in LGBTQ+ activities, never be victims, love their country, and never entertain Marxism. To the political Left, this is an anathema. Children must be groomed to indulge in anti-social, anti-Christian, and anti-American activities.

To recruit children for their nefarious activities, the political Left and organized crime must groom recruits starting at the earliest possible date.

The masters of the political Left in Moscow had already developed, perfected, and launched the model for grooming and brainwashing children against their parents and their God. The Soviet morality tale of Pavel Trofimovich Morozov was a perfect grooming tool for the Left. Born on November 14, 1918, and died on September 3, 1932, Pavel was born a year after the Russian Revolution. He was born to poor peasants in the small town of Gerasimovka. His father, Troflim, was chairman of the Village Soviet. Pavel was a supporter of Stalin. He was also the leader of the Young Pioneers, a dedicated Communist, and supported Stalin's collectivization of farms in the Soviet Union. However, Troflim was a traitor. He had been forging documents and selling them to enemies of the Soviet Union. Paval reported his father to the Political Police. His father was arrested, tried, and executed.

Of course, Pavel's family didn't appreciate Pavel's actions. As retribution, his uncle, grandfather, grandmother, and cousin murdered him and his younger brother. Afterward, all of them, excluding his uncle, were rounded up and executed by firing squad.

Young Pavel was designated a glorious martyr and hero of the Soviet Union. Statues of him were built and sent to almost every town in the country. The school that he attended became a shrine, and children from all over the Soviet Union were taken to see it. Most importantly, every schoolchild was told the story of Pavel and told that they were expected to emulate him.

The children of the Soviet Union were told that they were expected to do as Pavel had. Public education was commandeered to groom minor children to betray the laws of God or nature, their parents, and family and choose the government as their overlord, even if it meant their parents' death or their own.

In grooming the children of America to accept LGBTQ behavior, critical race theory, gender reassignment, pedophilia, victimization, and hate, the political Left must follow the playbook of its Communist masters and use their example of Pavel. They must teach the children that the state is everything. God, family, parents, and self are irrelevant. This grooming has been in full effect for decades, and the Left will not stop until we make it.

Borrowing a technique from convicted pedophile Jeffrey Epstein and convicted child recruiter, groomer, and pimp Ghislaine Maxwell's playbook, the Democratic Party has decided to become the groomer, recruiter, and pimp for the perverts on the political Left. On June 4, 2022, the *Washington Post* published a piece verifying that the Democratic Party–controlled public education system is now commandeered to groom and recruit America's children, making them active participants in the LGBTQ+ lifestyle. The piece by Laura Meckler is titled "How schools are learning to teach gender identity" and reads:

> Resources and lesson plans for those who want to teach about gender identity are becoming much more common. Seven states now require that curriculums include LGBTQ topics. The National Sex Education Standards, developed by experts and advocacy groups, name gender identity as one of the seven essential topics, alongside puberty, consent, sexual orientation, and other subjects. And the federal government recommends that schools include gender identity in their sex education programs.

There are three things that every free American should be offended and outraged about in this article: (1) There is a National Sex Education Standards group, (2) this National Sex Education Standards group was developed by experts and "advocates," and (3) the Democrat-controlled federal government is an advocate of gender identity education in the public education system.

On July 9, 2022, the *Washington Post* carried an article written by Hannah Natanson titled "LGBTQ clubs were havens for students. Now they're under attack." Natanson discussed a revolt by parents after learning that Gay-Straight Alliance clubs (GSAs) have been offered for over two decades in fourth and fifth grades and are being expanded without parental knowledge. When parents were alerted to the existence of these clubs, the school board in Maryville, Washington, proposed that "parental consent would be required for all non-curriculum student groups." This would make sense to any reasonable person. But the political Left is not reasonable. It has an agenda. Its secret plan was working. Now it was revealed and is being thwarted. In its anger, it revealed its true intent. This project was intended and needed to remain hidden from the prying eyes of meddling parents for it to be successful. Its proponents knew that sane parents would not allow them to corrupt their children. The story reads:

> This immediately raised fears, Panico said that LGBTQ kids in unsupportive homes would be "outed" to their families... The controversy in Maryville is part of a burgeoning nation-wide opposition to GSA club activities and in some places, their existence. These groups have been common and accepted in schools for two decades, offering a place for LGBTQ students and allies to gather. But now, some conservative parents and pundits, and politicians are alleging without presenting evidence that GSA clubs are sites of political indoctrination, where students are encouraged to assume LGBTQ identities without their parents' knowledge.

The piece continues:

> Near Monterey, Calif., Spreckels Union School District investigated and disbanded a mid-dle-school LGBTQ club after conservative activists criticized its advisers for helping students explore their identities, sometimes without parental supervision. In at least two school districts, one in Iowa the other in Pennsylvania,

administrators launched investigations and in the latter case suspended GSA advisers when the clubs hosted after-school drag performances.

Alexander Solzhenitsyn said, "The simple step of a courageous individual is not to partake in the lie." Some parents in Loudon County, Virginia, have complied. Indeed, on June 29, 2022, Fox News reported:

> The America First Legal, through its Center for Legal Equality has filed a lawsuit against Loudon County Public Schools for the district's systemic and egregious moral corruption of children and its deliberate, and almost gleeful, violation of parental rights to control the upbringing of their children... Some of the policies targeted in the America First Legal lawsuit, which the group noted was "on behalf of eleven courageous parents," include Policy 8040 and Regulation 8040, which the group said, "compels student speech, forces young children to use bathrooms and locker rooms with members of the opposite sex, and keeps parents in the dark when their children lead a double life as a different gender during school hours."

As I have stated previously, like organized crime, the Democrat-controlled federal government of Joe Biden, Nancy Pelosi, Chuck Schumer, and Jim Clyburn are nothing more than pedophile pimps for the political Left.

This pimping and grooming process has been quite successful. The *Post* piece continued,

But an increase in the number of young people identifying as trans or gender-nonconforming has prompted many schools to change course and adopt lessons that would have been unthinkable just a few years ago. A Gallup survey released last year found 16 percent of young adults in Generation Z identify as LGBTQ, more than any other generation.

For those of you who might think I am being hyperbolic, I submit to you Natanson's *Post* piece. If true, sane parents all of America should demand the dismantling of the public education "slavery" system, replacing it with a system of education freedom, including vouchers, charters, tax credits, grants, and scholarships. The story continues,

The approaches vary, particularly for elementary school children. In some classrooms, lessons about gender identity focus on gender stereotypes.

Students in first grade, for instance, may be prompted to consider that there are no "boy colors" or "girl colors. Some classes use the book "I Am Jazz," the story of a transgender girl. "I have a girl brain but a boy body," she says. "This is called transgender. I was born this way!"

A lesson meant for first grade called "Pink, Blue and Purple" comes from a curriculum called "Rights, Respect, Responsibility" developed by the activist group Advocates for Youth. It tells students that gender is not a fixed attribute.

> "You might feel like you're a boy even if you have body parts that some people might tell you are 'girl' parts," the teachers are told to say, "You might feel like a girl even if you have body parts that some people tell you are 'boy' parts. And you might not feel like you're a boy or a girl, but you're a little bit both. No matter how you feel you're perfectly normal!"

The sickness and evil of these people are so pervasive that they do not believe that they are doing anything wrong. They are completely anti-social, possessing reprobate minds. It is painfully obvious that the current educational system is populated with people that are either evil, stupid, or insane. Either way, from its admission to sexually grooming children for the sexual exploits of the political Left, teaching children to hate with critical race theory, or refusing to protect our children from mass shootings, the current public education system has proven that it deserves to be dismantled.

In Virginia, on September 20, 2022, newly elected Governor Glenn Youngkin issued new policies on transgender students, and the leftist Democrats lost their minds.

The new policies require parental approval for any changes in students' "names, nicknames, and/or pronouns," direct schools to keep parents "informed about their children's well-being," specify that student participation in activities and activities shall be based on sex and state that "students shall use bathrooms that correspond to his or her sex, except to the extent that federal law otherwise requires."

Democrats were outraged; it is well known that President Biden, Obama, Pelosi, Clyburn, and the entire crime family are all champions of sexually grooming children through public education. According to a September 20, 2022, piece in the *Washington Post*, some school districts in Democrat-controlled areas of Virginia are so hellbent on making sex objects out of small children that they are refusing to comply. Some even threatened to sue. That is the extent of their dedication to this evil task.

Like organized crime, there is a virulent anti-social and anti-American pathology among the members of the political Left, especially in the inner cities where Democrats have absolute control. Andrew Breitbart said, "Politics is downstream from culture," and brainyquotes.com says Thomas Wolfe wrote, "Culture is the arts elevated to a set of beliefs." Therefore, if you control the arts (education, TV, music, print media, social media), you control the culture. If you control the culture, you control politics. For this reason, government education is the battlefield of America's future, and its reform or destruction must be accomplished.

I do not believe that government education can be reformed. As with parents and children, there is this natural tension between citizens and their government. Government is that petulant rebellious child that will lie, cheat, or resort to any kind of pressure to extract concessions from the parents—the citizens. Like the child, the goal of the government is to dominate the parent, and the best way to achieve this goal is to educate the parent to obey the instructions of the child. Democrats have achieved this control through over sixty years of forced government public education inflicted upon American citizens. And it will never voluntarily give it up.

Science fiction writer Philp K. Dick stated, "The basic tool for manipulation is the manipulation of words. If you can control the meaning of words, you can control the people who must use them."

The political Left has even been successful at teaching the citizens of the United States to incorporate its vocabulary as the accepted nomenclature. We now call the physical castration of boys "gender-affirming care." We call tax increases "investments." We call the racist indoctrination of children "critical race theory." Instead of saying that elected government employees are our servants, we now call them leaders. This last example of nomenclature control is sacrilege to a free American and is the equivalent of parents calling their children mom and dad. This explains why the government treats us as children, and most Americans treat our government as our parents. Free people do not tolerate being led. We must teach our children the correct nomenclature. Our government employees, from the president to dog catcher, are "servants." We, the people, are the leaders.

Organized crime retained control of its members through isolation, fear, and a demented loyalty that transcended all logic and reason. It developed an "us against them" mentality against all outsiders. This isolation afforded these crime bosses a grand opportunity to indoctrinate their young members with an anti-social, hate-filled, criminal mentality that justifies every cruel action they are willing to partake in.

The most elite leaders in the Democratic Party emulate this plan to perfection. When rich white Democrats controlled the South, they isolated it from the rest of the world, turning it into a gladiator arena where they enticed poor white and black Americans to hate and kill one another for their amusement.

Most poor whites got wise to the exploitation and finally rejected the sick machinations of the rich Democratic elites and left the party. In a sick display of the most twisted logic in American history, the political Left told the world and convinced most blacks that Southern whites who left the racist Southern Democratic Party in the 1960s and 1970s and joined the anti-racist Republican Party did so because the Southern white Democrats who left were in fact racist. But if these Southern whites had remained loyal to the slaveholding, Jim Crow, Democratic Party of Bull Conner, and George Wallace, they would not have been racist.

It was Ionian philosopher Heraclitus who said, "Those unmindful when they hear, for all they make of their intelligence, may be regarded as the walking dead." I am reminded of this statement whenever it occurs to me that most black Americans have remained steadfast and loyal to the ways and politics of their old Democratic masters. While the lives of the whites that left this party of hate got much better, the lives of the blacks that stayed got tremendously worse. Like the bosses in organized crime families, white liberal Democrats have completely isolated and groomed them and many guilt-ridden white Americans. They control what they see, eat, and hear. The Democrats and the political Left control their education, religion, economy, politics, and arts. They are as isolated and as controlled today as they were during the days of the old antebellum South. Thus, blacks and guilt-ridden whites are easily groomed by their white masters to be compliant with any and all demands. Fear of the white Republican/conservative is an absolute necessity for this control. Even though this fear is completely irrational, the grooming process has taken hold.

In 2019, the FBI reported that 566 blacks had killed whites, while 246 whites had killed blacks. Nevertheless, in a May 18–20, 2022, *Washington Post*–Ipsos poll, 75 percent of black Americans reported that they are worried that they or someone they love will be physically attacked because they are black. In the same poll, seven in ten black Americans stated that at least half of white people hold white supremacist beliefs, and 65 percent believed that it is a bad time to be black in America. Thus, because of their isolation and control of the black community, Democrats have groomed most black people into believing that white conservatives have nothing else to do except sit around concocting plans to make black lives miserable, and the white Democrat is the only thing that can protect them.

Just as ridiculous are the condescending beliefs of those millions of white liberals with the temerity to believe that black people are the responsibility of white America and of the black Americans who believe the same. This ideology is the real racism. Democrats have convinced themselves and most blacks of the ability of white Americans to mold anything into their desired image, and if something is not molded, it is lacking, simply because enough white people have decided not to do it.

Liberal Democrats even choose the heroes of the black community. Through the manipulation of the arts, they have placed criminals in positions of high esteem. Like everything else, they choose the worst of our community for us to emulate. Like John Gotti and Jesse James are heroes of organized crime, Marxists, and gang leaders like George Jackson (founder of the Black Guerrilla Family street gang), Stanley Tookie Williams (founder of the Crips), Mumia Abu-Jamal (convicted cop-killer), Felix Mitchell (Oakland drug lord), and Huey Newton (suspected drug kingpin and murderer) are provided hero worship by the political Left. This worship is then reinforced culturally and thereby defines the Democratic Party and black community.

All of these men were a menace to their communities. They were nothing more than cultural suicide bombers for white liberals on the political Left. All dying young, leaving nothing but ruin in their wake. Most of this ruin was conducted in their own community among their own people. Because it is the intent of the political Left to groom your children to take the place of these gangsters. As the Palestine Liberation Organization (PLO) celebrates its literal suicide bombers, today, the political Left exalts and honors these men who murdered, terrorized, and all died young or will spend their lives in dark, dank prisons. Nevertheless, all is forgiven because they hated America, and they were Marxists. They are now just pictures on walls and names on tombstones in cemeteries and suicide bombers for white liberals at the Democratic National Committee, in Manhattan and in Hollywood.

The grooming and recruitment continue unabated. Every murderous Marxist traitor infiltrated into the black community has been lionized, elevated, and celebrated in the art of the political Left. The political Left has created a subculture where these suicidal attributes are nurtured, celebrated, and rewarded. Some of the most celebrated artists in the world have produced movies, songs, books, artwork, plays, museums, statues, and poems—Bob Dylan, Mario van Peebles, Tupac Shakur, and Snoop Dogg have all celebrated these murderers and have participated in recruiting our children for the political Left. To groom American children into accepting an anti-American, anarchist, and Marxist ideology is why they do this. Meanwhile, every builder and patriot, from Supreme Court Justice Clarence Thomas to Booker T.

Washington, is either lambasted or completely canceled into anonymity.

The grooming process continues as heroes are redefined as traitors, and traitors are defined as heroes. How can a society succeed in this type of dysfunction? It can't. It is meant to be dysfunctional. Through the union-controlled Marxist public education system, it is designed to implode.

In an April 22, 2022, op-ed, George Will wrote about the Democrats' willingness to sacrifice poor minority students to their funders in the teachers' unions. He wrote:

> There is an honor, of a sordid sort, in the Biden administration's showing more gratitude to a major donor than concern for the needs of millions of children, disproportionately minorities.
>
> The administration prefers the donor, a government-employees union, over the children, even though this tawdry fidelity to a funder will exacerbate Democrats' growing problems with Black and Hispanic voters. This is the significance of the number 97.9.
>
> From 1990 on, that is the lowest percentage of the American Federation of Teachers' campaign contributions that went to Democrats. It explains the administration's contemptible pettiness in persecuting charter schools with punitive regulations intended to be crippling.

Organized crime syndicates like the MS-13 and the Democratic Party start the grooming process of their victims while they play as children in the streets and at the schools of mostly Democrat-controlled ghettoes and economically depressed areas of this nation. In these areas, the father that provides the security, discipline, spiritual guidance, and sustenance for his family has, in most cases, either been imprisoned, killed, or mentally castrated. Once removed, these children are at the mercy of these forces of evil.

Understand: Either sick people or evil people seek to indoctrinate children into a belief system alien to that of their parents. To maximize their efforts, these people gravitate to public education as pedophiles gravitate to playgrounds. The inevitable result of such indoctrination is chaos in the home, leading to the utter destruction of the child and the family.

Children are turned into prideful neurotics, always looking for the approval of strangers instead of parents, and are, therefore, eternally unhappy. They are perfectly conditioned to join organized crime families, becoming self-loathing Democrats in this condition.

It is a satanic man or woman that turns a child against their God and their parents. These beasts demand that the children hate themselves by demanding that children pridefully question their gender, while these evil adults prepare them for sexual and political exploitation. Contrary to their slogans, it is never about the enrichment and emancipation of the child. It is about the only two things that criminal thugs and Democrats (I am redundant) care about: perverted sex and power.

On April 6, 2022, Laura Ingraham relayed a great report on her Fox News show explaining the Left's plans:

> By the time the children get into middle school, they
> are bombarded by efforts to undo any semblance

of traditional values their parents might have taught them. Teachers and administrators often, with fun personalities, are eager to share their experiences with gender identity.

These people in the public education system encourage small children to discuss their genitalia with them, question whether their biological sex is accurate, choose pronouns outside of "he" and "she" that coincide with how they feel instead of who they are, and whether they feel they want to have sex with boys, girls, or both.

It is simple: To get children to become more comfortable having sex with adults, one must first convince children to have a level of comfort discussing sex with strangers. From the openly LGBTQ+ and same-sex-married leader of the American Federation of Teachers, Randi Weingarten, to the array of sexually promiscuous libertines that have been invited into the ranks of many excellent public school teachers, public education is completely discredited.

This is too easy to fix. Teach the children ABCs, 123, and basic nonsexual history and send them home. Designate the parents with teaching the rest. But organized crime will not allow it. The separation of children from the loving eyes of their parents is the perfect opportunity for those that mean harm to do harm. Those that do not mean harm will always act in plain view of the loving parent and never in the shadows.

The sexualization of children is nothing new. Perverts and pedophiles have participated in the grooming and sexualization of small children for centuries. Democrats have been sexualizing and raping little black boys and girls since their party's inception in 1800. So, when the perverts in America decided that they needed more victims to fulfill their immoral sex cravings, they bundled their money and hired the Democratic Party to order the public school system to establish a grooming system solely designed for that purpose. This was not a hard sell. Hollywood pornographers have long been the top financiers of the Democratic Party. Joe Biden's election falsely convinced this cabal of perverts that they had a mandate from the American people to groom their children for their sexual pleasure.

"Drag Queen Story Hour," "bathroom bills" allowing boys into girls' bathrooms, and elementary school books like *Heather Has Two Mommies* and *My Two Daddies* tipped parents off to the conspiracy. Of course, the Democrats denied any conspiracies, but when Florida passed the Parental Rights in Education Act or what Democrats falsely call the "don't say gay" bill, all hell broke loose. Fatigued at being the Democratic Party's "side piece," it's their perverted financiers at the Human Rights Campaign that forced the Democrats to defend their sick policy agenda in the whole light of day. Now America knows.

We all agree that there are some great public school teachers in our schools, but they are not strong enough to deter this storm. Along with other hidden agendas to encourage race hatred, self-hatred, and national hatred, like critical race theory, the 1619 Project, and systemic racism, the public education system has become a willing partner in the Left's organized crime family.

The public may be aware now, but the damage to generations of children may have already been done. Gallup reported that Americans who self-identify as LGBTQ+ have exploded. Among baby boomers, born between 1956 and 1974, only 2.6 identified as such; among Generation X, only 4.2 percent identify as such; among millennials, 10.5 percent identify as such; and among Generation Z, 20.8 percent self-identify as LGBTQ+.

Perverts in the Democratic Party have been grooming American children to abstain from virtue and engage in vice for decades. Monsters aren't born; they're made by beasts.

The expulsion of religion, discipline, parents, and patriotism from public education couldn't have had any other result. But organized crime and Democrats (I'm being redundant) forgot one crucial fact: there are still Christians in America. All of us are not asleep or compromised.

Children should be led by their parents and no one else. The Preamble to the Constitution says that our Constitution was designed so "We the People" could "ensure the blessings of liberty to ourselves and our posterity." Posterity is defined as "descendants." Nevertheless, there have been a number of Democrats, from former Governor of Virginia Terry McAuliffe to Nikole Hannah-Jones of the 1619 Project, who have pridefully stated that parents should not oversee their children's education. Indeed, on April 10, 2022, Christine Emba of the *Washington Post* defended the grooming of minor children by public education:

> It's (using the word grooming) a cynical exploitation of loaded language to make bad faith attacks. It's also a way for parents to control what their children hear, by making anything that they oppose—same-sex marriage, say, or gender fluidity—seem beyond the pale… Plus, parents aren't always right.

Karl Marx said, "Accuse your enemy of what you are doing, as you are doing it to create confusion." Right out of the Marxist playbook, Democrats accuse those on the political right of

QAnon conspiracy theories when they are the ones engaged in an actual conspiracy to sexualize and groom little children.

Like every criminal enterprise, the Democratic Party is cannibalizing itself. Because many on the Left, through drug abuse, murder, or suicide, are dying untimely deaths and either cannot or will not birth children, they are coming for your children, grandchildren, and unborn children. The symmetry is amazing. We conservatives must fight to save our children from unlawful organized crime (Crips, Bloods, Mafia, Triad, MS-13) and *lawful* organized crime—the Democratic Party.

The lowest depths of hell lay in wait for those who willfully harm children. They are the lowest form of life existing on this earth. Jesus held them in such contempt that he stated in Matthew 18:6,

> But whoever causes one of these little ones who believe in me to sin, it would be better for him to have a great millstone fastened around his neck and to be drowned in the depth of the sea.

I hope these criminals can swim. Well—maybe not.

CHAPTER 5

MURDER FOR HIRE

If anything in this life is certain, if
history has taught us anything, it
is that you can kill anyone.
Michael Corleone, *The Godfather II*

O n September 23, 2022, Fox News exhibited on air a billboard paid for by the Newsom for California Governor 2022 Committee that said, "NEED AN ABORTION? CALIFORNIA IS READY TO HELP. LEARN MORE AT ABORTION.CA.GOV." That statement by itself is appalling enough, but Gavin Newsom used Mark 12:31, "Love your neighbor as yourself. There is no greater commandment than these," as justification for the murder of children.

In *The Merchant of Venice*, Shakespeare wrote,

> The devil can cite Scripture for his purpose,
> An evil soul producing holy witness
> Is like a villain with a smiling cheek,

A goodly apple rotten at the heart.
O, what a goodly outside falsehood hath!

Anais Niv said, "We don't see things are they are. We see them as we are." Murder-for-hire is one of those things. Nothing is more demonic, anti-social, or gross than the willingness to take a human life for money, pleasure, or power. The derision is expanded exponentially when it is determined that the victim is an innocent child. A person's soul, or lack thereof, is revealed based on their view.

Are you loyal or a betrayer? Are you compassionate or cruel? Are you selfish or sacrificing? Do you fear man or God? This sifting provides the political Left with all the information it needs to recruit every psychopath in America. Leo Tolstoy said, "if you feel pain, you're alive. If you feel other people's pain, you're a human being." These Democrats do not feel the pain of others. This apathy, however, has given them an advantage when it comes to the ability to exterminate innocent human life.

Every evil organization exerts its authority through terror and violence. The political Left is no different. Votes are acquired through intimidation, bribery, and fraud. The people are controlled through fear, violence, poverty, and substance abuse. Ironically the political Left gets rich by demanding the government fund billions of dollars in programs to alleviate the conditions caused by themselves and organized crime.

The anger, vitriol, and madness exhibited by the political Left and the Democratic Party after the Supreme Court made it more difficult for them to kill unborn children when it overruled *Roe v. Wade* in *Dobbs v. Jackson Women's Health Organization* were very telling. The Left reacted like drug addicts forced into rehab. The option of not being able to murder children was unfathomable.

Like reluctant rehab addicts, they immediately sought ways around the system.

On July 11, 2022, on her MSNBC show, Rachel Maddow reported approvingly that the Political Left is so hell-bent on killing children that an abortion doctor intends to put an "abortion ship" in the Gulf of Mexico. Democratic Senator Elizabeth Warren has suggested putting abortion clinics in federal national parks. Some have even suggested putting these murder mills on Indian reservations. Indeed, on February 6, 2021, Catholic News Services reported that forty-eight Democratic senators blocked the passage of the "Born Alive" bill:

> The measure requires that, when a baby is born alive following an abortion, healthcare practitioners must exercise the same degree of professional skill and care that would be offered to any other child born alive at the same gestational age. It also requires that, following appropriate care, health care workers must transport the child immediately to a hospital.

Like those in organized crime, Democrats understand that you don't get paid unless there is proof of death. The hit must be carried out. Blocking the "Born Alive" bill guarantees that their murder quota will be filled.

These psychotics are not finished. They must continue to produce a revenue stream through murder. They must fulfill their bloodlust. They must find a way to kill. Americans, however, must continue to find a way to not only make abortion illegal but also make it unthinkable.

The destruction of the family, decades of sexually grooming children, greed, and the psychotic need of the "Political Left" to commit murder are just some of these maladies.

One of the more evil and cowardly ways Democrats and the Left model organized crime is the murder-for-hire industry. It is a primary stream of income enjoyed by organized crime families like the Mafia, MS-13, and the Democratic Party. Organized crime families have a crew of trained "hitmen" always at the ready to carry out murder on demand for money. If you have the money, they have the bullet. These hitmen will kill anyone. The people they kill have not been afforded due process of the law and have not been found guilty of any crime. These hitmen are evil, merciless, anonymous, and paid very well. It goes without saying, the head of the family always takes his cut.

Like its fellow branches of organized crime, the Democratic Party leadership has many professional hitmen at the ready, locked and loaded to kill undesirables for profit. Except, these hitmen are worse than those in the Mafia. And, they have the benefit of legal protection. They have in their possession a license to kill. They are called "abortion doctors." They are merciless, anonymous, and paid better than the assassins in any organized crime syndicate.

The most proficient murder organization in the history of the Mafia was a group of psychotics appropriately called Murder, Inc. Bugsy Siegel, Albert Anastasia, and Frankie Carbo were some of the better-known members. It is reported that Murder, Inc. was responsible for between four hundred and one thousand contract killings between 1929 and 1941.

In 2022, before five Supreme Court Justices ruled the pro-murder *Roe v. Wade* verdict unconstitutional, the political Left operated 1,671 Murder, Incs. in the form of abortion clinics in the United States. At their most proficient, the Mafia's one

Murder, Inc. killed ninety people per year for ten years. Today's political Left's 1,671 Murder, Incs. are much more proficient, killing approximately five hundred babies for each Murder, Inc. every year for the past fifty years. The Planned Parenthood website says each of these abortion clinics receives between $580 and $2,000 per abortion, and on October 21, 2020, in a story for the *Washington Post*, Paige Winfield Cunningham reported Planned Parenthood for 2018–2019 received $616.8 million from the federal government siphoned to it by the Democratic Party and RINOs (Republican in Name Only), making the entire nation complicit in their crimes.

While in power, Democrats exorbitantly fund Planned Parenthood and, when out, filibustered or find a couple of RINOs to block every attempt by conservatives to defund the murderous organization. Their commitment to murder is so complete that Democrats have even threatened to shut down the entire federal government if abortion is not federally funded, as they did in 2018.

On February 2, 2018, *Politico* reported:

> Congressional Republicans are giving up on years of promises to cut federal funding for Planned Parenthood as Democrats prepare to take control of the House, a major setback for the conservative movement after controlling both chambers of Congress and the White House for the past two years… But while the (Republican) House repeatedly passed measures stripping Planned Parenthood of federal funding over the past two years, the efforts died one after another in Senate. Planned Parenthood supporters Sens.

Lisa Murkowski (R-Alaska) and Susan Collins (R-Main) proved an effective block within the Republican caucus, and when Democrat Doug Jones (D-Ala.) captured Alabama's special election passage became impossible.

For protection, financing, and allowing them to operate, Planned Parenthood provides campaign contributions or kickbacks to the Democratic Party and its candidates for every "hit" or abortion it carries out, making it the actual crime boss of Murder, Inc. Indeed, on October 9, 2019, a CNN headline reported, "Planned Parenthood's political arm to spend $45 million on electing candidates backing reproductive rights." *The Hill* reported on January 16, 2020, "Planned Parenthood launched a $45 million campaign to back Democrats in 2020." The soldiers always kick "up" to the boss.

This encouragement of child murder from the political Left and the Democratic Party is bearing fruit. On June 16, 2022, in a piece titled "Abortions in the U.S. rose in 2021, ending decades-long decline, report says," the *Washington Post* reported on a Guttmacher Institute study celebrating the increase in abortions in 2021 as something to be celebrated. It said,

> [An] increase in abortion numbers is a positive development if it means people are getting the health care they want and need, the report stated.
>
> "Rather than focusing on reducing abortion, policies should instead center the needs of people and protect their right to bodily autonomy."

In the same piece, Marjorie Dannenfelser, president of Susan B. Anthony Pro-Life America, subscribed the increase in abortion to the Democrats and the Biden Administration:

> "The Biden administration and Democrats in Washington push abortion on demand until birth, paid for by taxpayers-including dangerous mail-order abortion drugs." The story continued, "Guttmacher attributed the increase to a variety of factors, including some states' expansion of Medicaid coverage for abortions."

This expansion in Medicaid made it easier for poor women to abort children while making all Americans pay for them, and therefore complicit in murder, without their knowledge or consent. The Hyde Amendment passed on September 30, 1976, barring the use of federal money for abortion except for cases of incest, rape, or to save the life of the mother is no more. The Medicaid expansion demanded by the Democrats made it possible for the states to bypass the Hyde Amendment by providing the states with extra federal money thus freeing the states to utilize their own funds to murder poor children, most of them black. Now, according to a March 27, 2019, report by the Guttmacher Institute, 20 percent of all abortions, which is approximately 200,000 per year, are paid for by you, the American taxpayer. Whether you like it or not, the Democratic Party has made this entire nation complicit in child murder.

Compared to the Democratic Party's Murder, Inc., the Mafia and all other organized crime syndicates combined are mere amateurs. On August 30, 2019, a United Nations report on organized crime reported that from 2000 to 2017, organized crime had killed one million people worldwide. However, during that same time, the Democratic Party's Murder, Inc. murdered approximately 17 million children in the United States alone. The Guttmacher Institute reported in 2022 that 63 million children had been murdered by Murder, Inc., contracted by the political Left and the Democratic Party here in the United States of America since 1972.

Democratic support for abortion is about women's health is like the drug dealer's support for crack cocaine is about the addict's health. Like organized crime, the political Left and Democrats satisfy three needs through their Murder, Inc. subsidiaries: They make money from each hit. They satisfy a specific clientele. And most importantly, they gratify a psychotic bloodlust to commit murder. The money and clientele are minor; the need of the psychotics in the mob and the Democratic Party to shed innocent blood is the driving force behind everything that they do.

Understand, these psychotics would commit murder for free if they were alone. But to be able to legally kill millions of innocents under the protection of the Democratic Party while getting paid for it is all they could ever want.

The people of this country are so decent that they have difficulty believing this. But consider this, according to Britannica. com, during the worst and most violent calamity in world history, World War II, between 40 million and 50 million people died worldwide. When one considers this fact of history and its incomparable amount of evil—and then contemplates the amount of psychotic and inhuman savagery it would take to murder 63 million innocent children in America alone—one must conclude that the political Left and the people who allow themselves to be controlled by it are some of the most malevolent people to ever walked the face of this earth.

The political Left responded to the leaked Supreme Court decision overturning *Roe v. Wade* the way organized crime would have responded to a recalcitrant uncooperative mark. Its reaction was clothed in orchestrated criminality. From the orchestrated Supreme Court criminal leak, organized protests, and legislation to overturn the decision miraculously already written and ready for the Senate, the political Left amazed everyone with the efficiency of its crime machine. Its need to shed blood without prosecution while earning profit from it was on full display throughout the country with the crying, screaming, protesting, and gnashing of teeth.

In normal times, it would take the Democratic Party months to write legislation and introduce it to the Senate for a vote. In this instance, it did so in less than a week. Why? Thirteen states have trigger laws outlawing the murder of children if *Roe v. Wade* is ever overturned. This would perturb the Left's ability to commit murder and get paid for it legally. It also innately has the added irritant of saving the lives of babies.

But, even with this piece of legislation, the political Left exposed just how unhinged they are and how unscrupulous the already unscrupulous Democratic Party has become. The Left is so far gone that it cannot even acknowledge nature's creation. The act written by Democrats to protect the political Left's right to murder includes this sentence: "This Act is intended to protect all people with the capacity for pregnancy—cisgender women, transgender men, non-binary individuals, those who identify with different gender, and others."

Indeed, Democratic Secretary of the Treasury Janet Yellen implied at a Senate hearing on May 10, 2022, that poor black women would improve their lives if they aborted their children.

There is one positive outcome to the Left's meltdown over the Supreme Court's reversal of *Roe*. Its members' insane contempt for life and the need to commit murder has been displayed for the world to witness. They spray-painted on a Christian pregnancy-counseling center in Madison, Wisconsin: "If abortions aren't safe, you aren't either." Then they firebombed it. At Sunday Mass all over the country, pro-abortion terrorists interrupted services with morbid protests in costumes chanting about the need to murder children.

Tucker Carlson Tonight broadcasted a video of a pro-abortion activist in front of the Basilica of St. Patrick's Old Cathedral in New York City on May 8, 2022, simulating the birth of a child and then tearing a doll apart, screaming repeatedly, "I'm killing the baby. I'm killing the motherf&#king baby."

Fox News broadcasted a video of pro-abortion activists in front of a church singing, "Thank God for abortion." And abortion advocates are recorded protesting at the private homes of conservative Supreme Court justices, causing many of them to go into hiding. All of this is because the political Left is angry that it will no longer be able to profit from the murder of children in thirteen of the fifty states. Like the Mafia, the Crips, and the Bloods, the political Left is a death cult.

CHAPTER 6

♣

STEALING ELECTIONS &
CORRUPTING POLITICIANS

*I need Don Corleone, all those
politicians that you carry in your pocket
like so many nickels and dimes.*
Virgil Sollozzo, *The Godfather*

L ike members of organized crime groups, members of the
political Left love to steal and corrupt. It is their nature.
It is their passion. It is the reason they exist. Their inane
plans to defund the police, disarm the population, and end bail
are nothing more than a not-so-veiled attempt to transform the
United States into a Democratic Party heaven and an American
hell. The political Left has always admired Marxist states like the
USSR, Vietnam, and North Korea and through the Democratic
Party, it intends to create a kleptocracy identical to that of Russia
and Cuba, and a criminal dystopian narco-state in the image of
Afghanistan, Colombia, Mexico, Libya, and Nigeria.

Lysander Spooner asserted, "Those who are capable of tyranny are capable of perjury to sustain it."

Abraham Lincoln said as much about the Democratic Party when he warned in his "house divided" speech, delivered in 1858, that Democrats intended to enslave the entire nation. Nothing has changed. In 2021 they put forth their most valiant effort since the Civil War to bring that wish into reality.

To usher in this new age was the reason the presidential election of 2020 was likely stolen. It is my opinion that the election of 2020 was, indeed, stolen. How do I know? Because the Democrats and organized crime (tomato/tomahto) were involved in it. This is nothing new. In partnership with the criminal organization the Ku Klux Klan, the Democratic Party in the South has been stealing elections in earnest since free men were granted the right to vote in 1870. Like in a Mafia turf war, Democrats even stole elections from each other.

In his book *Means of Ascent*, Robert A. Caro describes how future President Lyndon Johnson fraudulently overcame a 20,000-vote deficit to defeat former Governor Coke Stevenson by eighty-seven votes in the 1948 Texas Democratic Party senate primary. Among other shenanigans, Caro wrote that a south Texas political boss named George Parr manufactured thousands of votes for LBJ.

On October 23, 2016, *Newsweek* reported that Earl Mazo, a Washington reporter for the *New York Herald Tribune*, and Pulitzer Prize–winning journalist Seymour Hersh wrote that John F. Kennedy stole the 1960 election from Richard Nixon in Illinois by utilizing the Daley machine in Chicago. In *Double Cross*, Sam and Chuck Giancana assert that Mafia Don Sam Giancana and Mayor Ricard Daley stole Chicago for Kennedy, thus stealing the entire state of Illinois and, therefore, the presidency, by fewer than one hundred thousand votes.

While running for a state senate seat in Georgia, future President Jimmy Carter lost the election to fraud perpetrated by Jim Hurst, chairman of the Quitman County, Georgia, Democratic Party for candidate Homer Moore. Carter challenged the result, proved the fraud, overturned the result, and won the rematch. These are just a few examples of the Democrats collaborating with organized crime to defraud the American people.

The entire Civil Rights Movement, including the 1964 Civil Rights Act and the 1965 Voting Rights Act, were necessitated because Democrats and their organized crime arm, the Ku Klux Klan, systematically murdered, intimidated, and beat black citizens to keep them from voting. When that did not work, Democrats installed literacy tests, poll taxes, and grandfather clauses.

In the north and big cities down south, the Democrats employed the services of the organized crime power of the political machine to build and maintain power. In New York, they utilized Tammany Hall; in Boston, the Kennedy machine; in Chicago, the Daley machine; in Los Angeles, the Bradley machine; in Missouri, the Prendergast machine; in Memphis, the Crump machine, and on it went. These machines control the black preachers, black civic organizations, unions, and gangs. They killed, bribed, and intimidated. These actions were not the activities of a political party. They are the actions of a criminal organization posing as a political party.

. In 2020, criminal organizations like Black Lives Matter and Antifa joined the ranks of the political Left, jolting the Democratic Party even further to the extreme. Beliefs and activities always suspected, but never admitted, are now part of the Democratic Party platform, and the Democrats used their criminal partners

BLM and Antifa to unleash the dogs of war upon the American people, initiating the greatest political fraud in American history.

Both BLM and Antifa are Marxist organizations. What is Marxism? Marxism is a political theory that advocates dictatorship, atheism, and the end of private property. Marxists advocate the end of freedom of speech, assembly, self-defense, press, religion, and privacy. Furthermore, they were willing to utilize violence and death to achieve this end.

According to a *Time* magazine article dated September 5, 2020, the Armed Conflict Location and Event Data Project (ACLED) analyzed more than 7,750 BLM demonstrations in all fifty states and Washington, DC, that took place in the wake of George Floyd's death between May 26 and August 22, 2020. The ACLED states that more than 2,400 locations reported peaceful protests and 220 reported violent protests. Logically that means that 5,150 were "not peaceful." We should add just add them to the 220 and call them violent. Therefore, there were 5,370 violent BLM demonstrations in the three months leading up to the presidential election year of 2020. According to Axios, on September 16, 2020, the BLM riots were the most expensive riots in American history, costing insurance companies between $1 and $2 billion. And devastatingly, according to an October 31, 2020, piece in *The Guardian*, at least twenty-five people were killed in these riots.

Activistfacts.com describes Antifa as:

> A militant, loosely organized movement of far-left vandals, rioters, and other criminals who advocate Marxism. The name Antifa, which is short for "anti-fascist," uses criminal violence to advance its causes, inflicting damage on innocent

civilians' property—a sign that the group is the
exact opposite of its name.

Death, destruction, and thuggery, all set against an innocent
American population, were designed to frighten and intimidate the American people into electing a mentally incompe-
tent Democratic president and a morally debased Democrat-
controlled Congress.

The fact that organized crime and the political Left have
collaborated to corrupt every pristine institution in American
society for profit, power, or just plain malevolence is a tragedy.
The electoral process, the hallmark of American democracy, has
been corrupted for the Left's benefit. Maybe in a way, we have
yet to realize we already live in the midst of Marxism; dictatorship already exists because elections are stolen. A new favorite,
LGBTQ+ rights have overtaken religion as the paradigm of virtue in American life. Family and biological sex no longer have
definitions. Standards of right and wrong have flipped. Sex and
violence corrupt the arts. Censorship, hatred, envy, and victimization have replaced aspiration in far too many Americans. The
political Left calls this carnage "progress."

This carnage was on full display in Dinesh D'Souza's movie
2,000 Mules. In it, the Democratic Party is caught red-handed
subverting democracy by collaborating with the criminal BLM
and Antifa organizations by delivering approximately 380,000
illegal votes to drop boxes in contested states during the 2020
presidential election.

As the press continually gaslights the American people by
telling them that there is no evidence of "widespread" voter fraud
and that Trump and his people keep pressing the "big lie" of election fraud, evidence abounds everywhere. And these Marxist

dictator wannabees continually ask us: Are you going to believe us or your lying eyes? Anti-Trump Harvard law professor Laurence Tribe tweeted:

> Donald Trump came within 43,000 votes of being re-elected even though Biden won by 7 million votes. We're asserting that it is a fact that 43,000 votes out of approximately 20 million could have swung the election in Wisconsin—20,608, Georgia—11,799, and Arizona—10,357. That is approximately 0.05 percent of the vote.

To understand how masterful and precise this theft needed to be, Aaron Blake concluded his analysis in the *Washington Post*: "In fact, Republicans came at most, 43,000 votes from winning each of the three levers of power." Thus, the fraud didn't have to be widespread. The Democrats could steal 43,000 votes out of 20 million in their sleep.

For the past 150 years, Democrats have utilized these tactics to win elections. However, this is the first time they have ever been caught red-handed on film working in an organized concert as a criminal conspiracy. The digital finger print of cell phone data has confirmed their guilt.

Even in their clumsy attempt to discredit the election of Donald Trump in 2016, Democrats let slip what many Americans long suspected. Voting machines that Democrats control in many big cities are untrustworthy. Many Democrats gave expert analyses of how these machines can be hacked.

Congressman Adam Schiff said, "our voting machines are vulnerable."

Congresswoman Shelia Jackson Lee said, "Voting machines are susceptible to hackers."

Senator Amy Klobuchar said, "Voting machines could be hacked."

Senator Kamala Harris said the "voting machines could be hacked."

Senator Ron Wyden said, "They could be hacked."

Senator Mark Warner said that the machines "could be hacked." And so did many others.

CBN News reported, "New Mexico State University Law Professor David Clements, a former assistant district attorney on the southern border, says the evidence of wrongdoing in the 2020 election is far stronger than the drug cases he prosecuted. 'I've never had a case with this much evidence, with this degree of quality to the evidence in my entire career,' said Clements."

President Eisenhower said, "If a political party does not have its foundation in the determination to advance a cause that is right and that is moral, then it is not a political party, it is merely a conspiracy to seize power."

After all you've previously read, tell me: What is right or moral about the Democratic Party? The political Left, through the Democratic Party, stole the 2020 election with the intention of passing a series of laws that guaranteed that they would never lose power again. In a devious scheme, Democrats, to give themselves control of the House of Representatives in perpetuity, passed HR1 in 2021. If passed by Congress this legislation would give them control of all congressional redistricting and require taxpayers to pay for their congressional campaigns.

In total disrespect and disregard for American norms, American traditions, and the will of the American people, the Democrats devised a commission to study how they could pack the Supreme Court with justices burdened only with rubber stamping their illegal and destructive activities.

In an effort to blow up the Senate and give them total control with only fifty-one votes, the Democrats in the executive branch, the House, and the majority in the Senate have demanded that the Senate end the filibuster.

In 2021, Democrats passed the Equality Act labeling Christianity as discriminatory and revoking the 1993 Religious Freedom Restoration Act. Parts of Build Back Better would essentially give legal status to illegal aliens, and grant illegal aliens free community college while prohibiting Immigration and Customs Enforcement officers from deporting illegals.

On May 12, 2022, the Democrats got into the "dope game"—as a *New York Post* headline read: "Crack pipes given to addicts in 'safe drug' sites up for Biden $$$: report." The Biden Administration allowed the selling and consumption of illegal drugs, violated federal law by ignoring the federal "crack house statute," and embraced "harm reduction methods" that allow the operation of supervised injection sites of addictive and illegal drugs in American cities controlled by Democrats.

This conspiracy to seize power was the very reason some say the Democrats put so much effort into stealing the election in 2020, only to have it thwarted by one conservative Democrat from West Virginia, Joe Manchin, and one moderate from Arizona, Kyrsten Sinema.

Like organized crime, the political Left had initiated a plan to change the rules of government so that its members could cheat legally. In order to do this, they needed to eliminate the filibuster. No political party had ever seriously considered doing this before.

The filibuster was instituted in the Senate to guarantee the continuity of government. Without it, the very laws that were passed two years earlier could be rescinded and then repassed in an endless cycle of incompetent government. To end this cycle

of incompetence, the Senate decided that most pieces of legislation would no longer require fifty-one votes to pass but sixty.
With Kamala Harris as vice president, the Democrats possessed
fifty-one votes in the Senate and they wanted to wield that vote
to seize power in America and retain it forever. But they needed
all fifty-one Democrats to vote to eliminate the filibuster. Joe
Manchin and Kyrsten Sinema refused.

Therefore, the organized crime element of the political Left
was activated. These two senators were verbally harassed, stalked,
and publicly humiliated. Senator Sinema was even followed into
a bathroom and verbally assaulted while in the stall. This assault
was videoed, going viral across the internet.

The criminal elements in the black community, including
crooked black preachers, Marxist black civil rights organizations,
and black Democratic politicians, all went to the streets demanding an end to the filibuster so that the political Left could pass
$6 trillion in Build Back Better funding, Democratic Party con-
trol of federal elections, packing of the Supreme Court, adding
Washington, DC, and Puerto Rico as states (which would add
four more Democrats to the Senate), and force religious institutions to accept LGBTQ+ indoctrination.

The governors of each state are given the power to appoint a
replacement if a senator dies in office. The governors of Arizona
and West Virginia are Republican. The anger against these two
Democrats is so extraordinarily violent that I am persuaded that
this is the only reason Senator Manchin and Senator Sinema
have not met an untimely demise.

The political Left and organized crime stealing elections
and thus corrupting our system of government is possibly their
most sinister and dangerous kinship. Usually, in organized crime,
there is a code. It says that people not "in the game" should not be

affected. However, stealing elections and corrupting the political process violate that code by taking advantage of innocent citizens who have never gambled, used drugs, sought out a prostitute, or even broken a minor law. The political Left targets and hurts the innocent. Therefore, we as citizens must be ever vigilant.

CHAPTER 7

♣

ADDICTION/DEPENDENCE

Sonny Corleone: *The niggers are having
a good time with our policy banks up
there in Harlem, driving them new
Cadillacs, paying 50 percent on a bet.*
Carlo: *I knew that was gonna start happening
as soon as they started making a lot of money.*
The Godfather

Ain't no money like dope money.
Tommy "Buns" Belly

•

A ddicting a victim to a product that can be provided only by
the crime group is a staple of the organized crime market-
ing model. Whether it be drugs, gambling, prostitution, or
the protection rackets, crime groups monopolize, control, addict,
and abuse.

The Democrats have perfected this section of the organized crime model. I have proof that, like organized crime, the

Democratic Party is nothing more than a drug pusher, addicting black people, and now all of America, to the crack cocaine of welfare, sloth, and government dependence. Furthermore, this addiction has been multigenerational in its design, with plans to be never-ending. In his book *And the Walls Came Tumbling Down*, Rev. Ralph Abernathy, successor to the Rev. Dr. Martin Luther King, Jr., and president of the SCLC, recognizing the havoc that welfare dependence was wreaking on the black community, wrote about the time that he approached the Democratic Party in an attempt to stop it:

> I decided to develop a model program to help black people break the chains of welfare and find new freedom in self-sufficiency... But as soon as I began to investigate the prospects for government funding, I discovered a curious thing: A good many people in government were quite happy with the status quo.
>
> They liked the idea of a huge, economically dependent population. The fact that there were third-generation welfare families pleased them.
>
> I was a life-long Democrat, but many Democrats I knew were satisfied with the welfare system and saw it as a benign thing rather than as a millstone around the neck of the black population. They too readily accepted the unchallenged assumption that the people on welfare were unwilling and/or unable to support themselves and that the situation in our urban centers was insoluble.

So long as our people continued to support the Democrat party, its leaders would make no attempt to change the system. For them, it was working all too well.

This information is from one of the icons of the Civil Rights Movement. To most sober people this information would be enough for them to leave the Democratic Party forever. But information like this doesn't matter to addicts. And most black Democrats are addicted to the "D." As a matter of fact, Speaker of the House Nancy Pelosi, while holding a glass of water and speaking of the absolute control the Democrats have over minority communities, on April 16, 2019, *Daily Mail* quoted her as saying, "This glass of water would win with a 'D' next to its name in those districts." Amazingly it did not matter to most black Democrats that Nancy was their pusher and they were the "junkies." Was she telling the truth?

Why would the Democratic Party and the political Left covet a community saddled with addiction? Because they want control. While good people trust free will and freedom while shunning control and celebrating choice, bad people must win through force while maintaining control via fear and addiction.

We can show American parents' irrefutable evidence that the government education system is sexually grooming their children, fomenting race hate and self-hate through critical race theory. We can even prove that their children are receiving the worst educational instruction in the industrialized world.

Nevertheless, because many parents are addicted, it does not matter. The addiction to the crumbs that fall from the Democratic Party table and the lie that one can lead a consequence-free life supersedes all other rational thought. Hardcore Democratic supporters' rejection of natural law necessitates that they find some other earthly law to imprint upon and entrust all of their hopes and aspirations. The false promises of protection from imaginary enemies along with the Democratic Party's arrogance, in telling the gullible that they could fill the subconscious need of all human beings to never want or fear anything again is the false opiate enticing the absolute loyalty of those who no longer trust in God or believe in natural law.

Like organized crime, the political Left uses addiction as a weapon. Not just addiction to drugs, prostitution, porn, or gambling—also to hate, envy, victimization, and free government stuff. Addiction has a duality to it; it is both comforting and distressing. It is also without control, completely emotional, and void of humanity.

The seven chief virtues of the political Right, even if not always followed, are humility, charity, chastity, gratitude, temperance, patience, and diligence. These aspirations are the complete opposite of the seven vices, usually always followed, of the political Left—pride, greed, lust, anger, gluttony, envy, and laziness. These vices are also associated with the behavior of addicts.

Addicts are concerned with "me." "My" emotions, "my" feelings, and "my" needs. Merriam-Webster defines addiction as "a compulsive, chronic, physiological or psychological need for a habit-forming substance, behavior, or activity having harmful physical, psychological, or social effects and typically causing well-defined symptoms, such as anxiety, irritability, tremors, or nausea) upon withdrawal or abstinence."

Sobriety is the opposite of addiction. Sobriety is defined as "marked by sedate or gravely or earnestly thoughtful character or demeanor." All people should strive to be sober in their thinking, finances, emotions, and character. There is manliness and Christian virtue in sobriety. There is steadiness and control in sobriety. As we all strive to avoid addiction, we should run to embrace sobriety. Just as addiction is their friend, sobriety is the enemy of organized crime and the political Left.

Addiction turns grown men into stalkers, crybabies, and victims. These men are concerned with using people solely to fulfill their needs by force if necessary. These needs can be physical, psychological, real, or imaginary. But they are not Christian, manly, or virtuous. They are addicted, irrational, cowardly, and self-defeating, and all in the domain of organized crime and the Democratic Party.

Like an addiction to gambling and drugs, there is an addiction to the need for white approval among most black Americans, and a need for redemption from white Americans. The political Left feeds this addiction. Because this pain point in America is a relic of slavery, Democrats are masters at exploiting it because they were masters of the slaves when slavery was nurtured. This addiction is now cultural in nature and the Democrats are benefitting from it and therefore have no intention of altering it.

Through this addiction, the political Left and the Democratic Party have turned the black Democrats into a generation of stalkers and white liberals into a generation of enablers. The black community's addiction to integrating with and equality with white Americans has provided the Democrats with a problem for which they testify that they alone can solve. So, instead of helping black Americans improve their communities, neighborhoods, schools, families, and economies, they encourage them to stalk white America. Like organized crime, Democrats have always understood, that with self-improvement, Democrats lose control of the addict. The goal then was to keep the addict a junkie by supplying him, lying to him, and humiliating him. The pusher never intends to let the junkie off the hook.

Like organized crime, the Democrats on the political left have convinced Americans of all races, with a concentration on blacks, that addiction is virtuous activity. Fixing the addiction of many blacks to be near and affirmed by whites led to humiliating spectacles designed for blacks to force their way into white neighborhoods, schools, restaurants, and bathrooms.

Regarding the concept of black people marching, crying, and dying to forcibly integrate with white America by the barrel of a gun if necessary, heavyweight champion Muhammad Ali once said, "It is a sick mind that wants to be somewhere he's not wanted." This sick mind is diseased. It is addicted to the drug of "whiteness." And the Democratic Party is black America's pusher.

Consider the legend of the civil rights marches, boycotts, and sit-ins. Included in these made-for-TV events were *Brown v. Board of Education*, the Montgomery Bus Boycott, the Little Rock Nine, Ruby Bridges, and the Orangeburg Massacre.

The humiliation of six-year-old Ruby Bridges, having to sit in a school alone for a year while being insulted and threatened by white racists, and the Little Rock Nine being assaulted and accosted was insanity on full display. White parents pulled their children out of the schools and hurled insults at these children. One even exhibited a black baby doll in a coffin to Ruby Bridges. She was so hated and so despised by the parents of William Frantz Elementary School that she had to be escorted to school every day by United States Marshalls for her protection. The 101st Airborne was dispatched to Little Rock, Arkansas, to protect the Little Rock Nine. And Robert Coles, a child psychologist, provided weekly counseling to a traumatized Ruby Bridges.

This mass addiction to whiteness was also on full display in the Orangeburg Massacre, where three young black men were killed by police while attempting to integrate an all-white bowling alley in Orangeburg, South Carolina. This insanity continued with *Brown v. Board of Education*, through which millions of black children were forced to abandon a good education delivered by black teachers who protected and loved them only to be thrust into state schools operated by the old Confederacy and staffed by teachers, many of whom were admitted ad committed racists who hated them.

I take no pleasure in saying this, but these efforts at forced integration were in fact a litany of sad spectacles displaying an addiction within the black community so perverse that parents were willing to sacrifice their own children to get a fix. The political Left corralled all of these addicted, self-hating blacks into a voting block strong enough to take over the entire Democratic Party, transforming it from a party of white racism to a party of white racism and Marxism/Communism.

These parents who forced their children into this cauldron of hatred should have been charged with child abuse. Instead, the political Left holds them in high esteem because they believe in, support, and are presently engaged in child abuse. Furthermore, they need the permission of the children's parents to carry out their crimes. They, therefore, hold the parents of Ruby Bridges, the Little Rock Nine, and *Brown v. Board of Education* as perfect examples of what all parents should be: addicts willing to sacrifice their own children to their Democratic pusher to get their fix of whiteness.

Such visual displays of addiction, from self-flagellation, self-hatred, and acknowledgment of one's own worthlessness, had never been witnessed anywhere on the earth. And liberal white

Americans cheered because these actions dually verified why some whites wanted nothing to do with blacks and why others said that only the presence of white people could save blacks from their inferior slave-minded selves.

These images depicted in a positive light are very unhealthy. America has wondered out loud why black Americans have such a difficult time achieving success. Let me present an example. If envious stalkers, addicts, cowards, and beggars are paraded as heroes to children, whom will the children emulate? They will emulate envious stalkers, addicts, cowards, and beggars. Most black children educated in the past forty years in America have fulfilled that prophecy. Many, as adults, like their parents, have become envious stalkers, addicts, cowards, and beggars, still craving the approval of oppressors in the Democratic Party who hold them in absolute contempt.

For example, the current president of the United States, Democrat Joe Biden, is by all standards the worst president in American history. He is currently polling below 40 percent in every poll and has the lowest approval rating of any previous president. He supports everything black people are against—the confiscation of guns, government-funded abortion until birth, the sexual grooming of children through public education, and open borders. He is currently leading America into a recession with double-digit inflation. Biden called black American men "super predators" and in 1994 introduced the most racist and punitive crime bill in American history. It incarcerated millions of black men, decimating families and lives for generations. Biden even said that black people that do not vote for him "ain't black." Nevertheless, against all logic, in a poll reported by the *Washington Post* on June 5, 2022, 70 percent of black Americans gave Democrat Joe Biden a good job approval.

Also, after all of the crime, poverty, terrible schools, and drug abuse in black communities controlled by Democrats, the *Washington Post* reported in the same piece that "three-quarters of Black Americans say the Republican Party is racist against Black Americans; a quarter say the same about the Democratic Party." The only explanation for this behavior is a combination of mass insanity, mass stupidity, or mass addiction.

The only good news in this poll is that Biden's support is down.

Examine these heroes of the Civil Rights Movement and how history has been written to redefine irrational addiction and insanity into virtue.

Leftist historians have redefined the irrational and pitiful act of stalking into an act of bravery. They have rewritten the act of self-hatred into black pride. They have rewritten the act of child abuse into upward mobility.

These black people do not understand this, but like a drugged and addicted crackhead in any Democrat-controlled American city, during that time in history, they were viewed with either pity or contempt. And in an effort to keep black people on the crack pipe of integration, Democrats and many condescending whites still hold these addicts up as paradigms of virtue for us and our children to emulate.

During slavery and into Jim Crow, many black parents allowed whites to mistreat and sexually abuse them and their children. The all-black school was in fact a refuge from white oppression. But like a trained dog bringing the leash to his master before a walk, addicted parents chose the humiliation of slavery over the exhilaration of freedom. Because of the intense social pressure, any black Americans resisting the urge to give in to this addiction would have been miraculous. Why Ruby Bridges' parents, Abon and Lucille Bridges, were persuaded by the NAACP to remove their daughter from the comfort of an all-black school that loved her, into an all-white school that hates her strains congruity. Even as modern history attempts to portray this event as brave and of positive historical significance, I do not see how. This type of behavior from black people toward white Southerners was not novel. Close proximity to white people had been viewed as a form of capital since slavery.

What was accomplished? According to Measure of America, a nonprofit that maps opportunity and well-being in America, black education in New Orleans did not get better; it got worse. It reported that the education gap in New Orleans is three times higher than the gap across the rest of Louisiana. School segregation in New Orleans is a little better. In 2022, 9 percent of the children in the New Orleans public education system were white. I guess the black integrationists are elated. They've wrecked the education of black children but they can sit beside a few white children. What a trade.

Everything for most black people in New Orleans has gotten much worse. But they are celebrating. This past February, during Black History Month, I saw depictions and celebrations of Ruby Bridges and the Little Rock Nine everywhere. But what are they celebrating? According to WDSU TV, in 2022, New Orleans had the highest murder rate in the nation. So, what are they celebrating? The house negros in the Iron Triangle and the political Left are celebrating because black Americans are still addicted, and as Ralph Abernathy said, the Democrats still have control.

What is the difference between slavery and addiction? Nothing. Both compel you against your will. The political Left has added to these psychological addictions. The LGBTQ+ indoctrination and sexual grooming of children and forcing others into participating is another psychological addiction that the Democrats have skillfully exploited. They have convinced people who are addicted to pride, sexual deviancy, and the need for acceptance to hire them as their pushers. Democrats have promised to legalize and normalize their drug of choice while punishing fellow Americans who will not engage in their addictive activity.

Sobriety, the opposite of addiction, is the perfect condition for mankind. A friend of mine named William, who happens to be white and a son of the old South, one day told me a story I'd never forget. It was the story of a friend he had when he was a boy. His friend who happened to be black hated his blackness. He would verbally exclaim to William how much he hated being black and how he wished God had made him white. William would try to comfort him by telling him that God had made him black and that God did nothing wrong or ugly.

This young man fell in love with a white girl. When she rebuffed him, he came to William frantically cursing and hating his blackness and himself for being black. In the midst of his self-flagellation, he grabbed a nearby gun, put it to his chest, and shot himself in the heart. He died that day hating the color of his skin and himself.

William borrowed this anecdote to explain to me why he had learned to respect me. He said that I was the first black man he had ever met who never acted like a victim or inferior to him. All others to some degree had acted as the young black man in the story: addicted to envy, self-hate, and forcing white America to accept the presence of black people and responsibility for black failure. I do not engage in this ideology nor does anyone in my family.

I am a child of God. An heir of Jesus Christ. I am an American. And I am the opposite of an addict: I am sober and free.

Chapter 8

Trafficking

*Now we have the unions, we have the
gambling and they're the best things to have.
But narcotics is a thing of the future.
And if we don't get a piece of that action,
we risk everything, we have. I mean not
now, but, ah, ten years from now.*
Tom Hagen, *The Godfather*

Securing the border is the responsibility of
the federal government. "The United States
shall guarantee to every State in this Union a
Republican Form of Government, and shall
protect each of them against invasion, and on
Application of the [state] Legislature, or of
the Executive (when the Legislature cannot
be convened) against domestic Violence.

Section IV, Article 4, United
States Constitution

Future Mafia Don and future boss of the Gambino crime family Carlo Gambino illegally entered the United States of America on December 23, 1921, as a stowaway on the SS *Vincenzo Florio* at Norfolk, Virginia. Lucky Luciano legally migrated from Sicily, settling on the Lower East Side of Manhattan in April 1906.

Immigration has brought some of the greatest and most productive people to the shores of this nation. It has also brought some of the most destructive.

Mexican cartels make billions of dollars transporting drugs, people, arms, and terrorists into America. They spend millions hiring lawyers and bribing politicians and law enforcement. In America, there is a legal way to bribe politicians. It is accomplished through the long-accepted skullduggery of lobbying.

Lobbying firms cannot bribe politicians directly. So, they've found a way around it. Lobbying firms hire relatives of politicians, paying them exorbitant fees for excess and influence on their political relatives. Instead of paying the politician, they pay the politician's spouse, children, or siblings. If you want to understand why the US government is in violation of its constitutional duty and will not secure its own border, do not look any further.

In a May 4, 2015, essay titled "Drug Cartels and Business," Timothy Klein wrote, "Since 2004, there have been 138 convictions or indictments in corruption investigations involving members of the United States Customs and Border Protection." He also reported that research suggested that the United States had given favorable status to the Sinaloa cartel, protecting its leaders and its operations in order to receive information on rival drug cartels.

Before being thwarted by public outcry, how do you think the Biden Administration was talked into providing $450,000 to illegal immigrant families who separated as they attempted to enter the country illegally? Have you ever considered why, on April 14, 2020, Virginia Governor Ralph Northam was convinced to join nineteen other states in signing a law giving in-state tuition to illegal aliens? Why do you think Democratic Senator Dick Durban blocked an amendment proposed by Republican Senator Ted Cruz, denying COVID-19 stimulus checks to illegal immigrants, as reported by *Newsweek* on March 8, 2021? Lobbying.

Trafficking is one of the essential activities of organized crime and the Democratic Party (but I repeat myself). Trafficking is the transportation or movement of illegal material or human beings for illegal actions. Sex-trafficking is human trafficking for the purpose of sexual exploitation. It has rightly been compared to slavery. The worst people in the world engage in this behavior. Democrats are tailor-made for this occupation.

Democrats consistently proclaim that they do not support illegal immigration. However, according to a March 22, 2021, study from the Center for Immigration Studies, there were eleven sanctuary states all controlled by Democrats (California, Colorado, Connecticut, Illinois, Massachusetts, New Jersey, New Mexico, New York, Oregon, Vermont, and Washington). Also, there were hundreds of sanctuary cities in these states. I cannot find one that is not controlled by Democrats.

On May 23, 2019, Republican Senator Pat Toomey from Pennsylvania introduced a bill in the Senate that would put an end to sanctuary cities in the United States. In February 2022, a majority of the Senate voted in support of the Stop Dangerous Sanctuary Cities Act, but it was filibustered by, you guessed it, the Democratic Party. According to a January 9, 2022, *New York Times* piece, the Democrat-controlled city of New York has even made it legal for more than 800,000 illegal aliens to vote in city elections until June 27, 2022, when New York State Supreme Court Justice Ralph J. Porzio struck it down.

Why would Democrats block a bill that would end sanctuary cities, knowing that these policies encourage illegal immigration and all of the destructive activities that come with it? Because they make money and secure political power through trafficking and illegal immigration.

As the New York City plot to empower illegals to vote, Democrats are bringing their future constituencies in through this illegal trade. One of the Democrats' most loyal constituencies is the LGBTQ+ community, which has procured asylum laws that let people into America, no questions asked except one: Are you LGBTQ? If the answer is yes, you get in. According to My Attorney USA, Democratic President Bill Clinton began allowing asylum based on homosexuality in 1994. In 2012, another Democratic president, Barack Obama, expanded it to "LGBTQI+." Yes, you read correctly; the political Left demanded the opening of, and Democrats opened, the floodgates of America to people all over the world based on how they have decided to have sex and whether they believe in biological gender.

Democrats will not secure the Mexican border because they are also involved in population trafficking. Population trafficking is a long-term game plan designed to bring as many poor, illiterate, and unskilled workers as possible to America. Democrats will then addict them to government programs and buy time with the hope that Democrats will one day achieve a supermajority in Congress that will give citizenship and the vote to these populations, or that they will be awarded a favorable Supreme Court victory that will give them both.

This plan was working well. Hillary Clinton was supposed to win the election in 2016 and place three liberal justices on the

Supreme Court. These justices would then vote to legalize more than 20 million illegal aliens, giving them the vote—and giving Democrats perpetual power. The election of Donald Trump and his subsequent placement of three conservative justices on the Supreme Court postponed Democratic plans for about twenty years. In the meantime, however, Democrats still intend to block all legislation that includes securing the border, building a border wall, or deporting illegals, thus bringing as many illegals as possible into America and playing for time.

"Hate America Trafficking" is something that the political Left depends on. Hatred for the values of our nation is a prerequisite item for consideration if the Democrats are to allow asylum. Radical Muslims, LGBTQ+ advocates, Communists, radical feminists, Marxists, murderers, and drug lords all receive asylum under Democratic immigration policies.

Immigrants who love America and our values, who obey our laws, who choose to assimilate, and who come here legally are hated and despised by the political Left and the Democratic Party. These legal immigrants come here to contribute, not to take. They come to conform to the American way, not to change it. They come here to protect, not to pillage. They are not dependable Democratic Party voters. For this reason, Democrats will continue to block every effort to pass any law to make *legal* immigration easier, and conservatives will block any law that will allow citizenship and the right to vote to those who come here illegally.

Sex-trafficking allows Hollywood moguls to make billions from the prostitution and porn that comes from it. These degenerates finance the Democratic Party and all their candidates.

Hugh Hefner of *Playboy* and Larry Flynt of *Hustler* were large contributors to the Democratic Party before their deaths. On March 27, 2005, UPI reported Larry Flynt as saying, "I've been a Democrat all my life." On August 14, 2000, the *New York Times* printed a story titled "The Democrats; Hefner's Record of Donations Reflects Their Liberal Ideology." In a May 13, 2011, article for CBS News, Hugh Hefner is quoted as saying,

> When Dr. King came to the Playboy Mansion he was in Chicago specifically to deal with the segregation that existed in Chicago. And that is how I met. Jesse and I was very actively involved after King's death in the funding of PUSH and the Rainbow Coalition.

Yes, you read correctly. Just when you thought that the character of these two could not go any lower you find that the Right Rev. Dr. Martin Luther King, Jr., and his protégé, the Right Rev. Jesse Jackson, spent time at the Playboy mansion ushering the once-maligned porn industry into the Civil Rights Movement, the Democratic Party, and American politics. And you can bet they were not at the Playboy mansion to save souls or to preach.

An October 12, 2018, piece in *The Hollywood Reporter* stated, "Hollywood has always been a reliable source of contributions to Democratic Party politicians and organizations, but perhaps never so more than the 2018 election cycle."

Oh, and don't believe that Democrats are too high-minded to accept money from and support child pornography. On October 16, 2009, a Mantecabulletin.com headline read, "Democrats' cozy dealings with NAMBLA." NAMBLA (the North American Man/Boy Love Association) is a silent partner of pedophiles in the Democratic Party that openly advocates for the repeal of all laws preventing grown men from having sex with minor boys.

On February 21, 2019, a story was written, accompanied by a poster with a picture of Barack Obama, with the words "NAMBLA for OBAMA" written on it, while being held by what seem to be two gay men. A March 24, 2019, headline on ExposingChristianError.Wordpress.com reads, "North American Man/Boy Love Association and the Democratic Party." The story chronicles the North American Man/Boy Love Association's support of the Democratic Party and asks why any Christian would support such an organization or party.

Now, for the big question: Why do all these perverted groups find their way to the Democratic Party? All these groups are part of the political Left. The political Left is also extremely wealthy. The Left needed a vehicle to transport their ideology into government and thereafter into law. The Democratic Party, for a price, will literally do anything and pass any law. To destroy America, the political Left purchased itself a political party to finish the work it started during the Civil War when it murdered over 800,000 citizens.

The Democratic Party continues to be a criminal organization in league with foreign criminal organizations such as Mexican coyotes and drug cartels. These organizations control human trafficking at the border, sex traffickers at the border, drug trafficking at the border, and population replacement of the American citizenry conducted at the border. And Democrats not only refuse to secure the border, but they also entice illegal activity.

CHAPTER 9

MORAL RELATIVISM

I work my whole life. I don't apologize to take
care of my family, and I refused to be a fool,
dancing on the string held by all those bigshots.

Vito Corleone, *The Godfather*

Friedrich Nietzsche wrote:

Morality is neither rational nor absolute nor natural.

The world has known many moral systems, each of which advances claims universality; all moral systems are, therefore particular, serving a specific purpose for their propagators or creators and enforcing a certain regime that disciplines human beings for social life by narrowing our perspectives and limiting our horizons... A moral system valid for all is basically immoral.

Working as a correctional officer at the Kirkland Correctional Institution in Columbia, South Carolina, it always amazed me that the inmates had the ability to justify any action, no matter how heinous. Being raised in a home where Christian values were absolute and instructed, and we were in a constant state of striving even though we regularly fell short, morality was not relative to me. It was an absolute. Therefore, my interaction with these men was troubling, educational, and fascinating. I understood why moral relativism is so dangerous.

Watching them in action, I would routinely ask the question: How could someone be so messed up? I routinely witnessed assaults, murders, gay orgies, gambling, and the occasional murder. The inmate always justified his action with some type of moral ambiguity.

Reading about the historical slavery, the Confederacy, Jim Crow, and black codes of the Democratic Party, and now the abortion, socialism, and atheism of the same, one must ask: How have the Democrats persisted as the oldest political party in the world? They lie.

The Hunter Biden laptop, the Big Steal 2020, the Antifa/BLM riots of 2020, the Russia hoax, COVID-19 protocols, drop boxes, mules, and ballot harvesting were all designed to allow Joe Biden to win the 2020 presidential election. It worked. Furthermore, Democrats are proud of it.

This moral relativism is a learned behavior. It was honestly received by inmates from people heaped in dysfunction and usually living in a dystopia. The peers and role models of these young men were usually the people most responsible for their moral demise. To them, I was abnormal and an emblem of curiosity. Conversely, I chose a peer group and role models that reflected my Christian beliefs and confirmed them. The inmates at Kirkland

Correctional Institution chose people who affirmed this moral ambiguity.

In order to mentally survive, members of organized crime needed this cognitive dissonance. The political Left mimics this behavior. George Orwell said, "They fear love because it creates a world they can't control." Organized crime and the Democratic Party covet control. Therefore, in order to survive, they cannot teach us to love one another. They believe that they must teach hate, envy, and moral relativism.

It is necessitated that their immorality, no matter how irrational, must be rationalized. But morality, by nature, must have an absolute standard-bearer from which rules and actions can be measured. For most Americans, these actions are measured from a mostly religious standard. For organized crime and the political Left, the religious standard is each individual person making the decision with his personal gratification as the only beacon of destination. Each person is a law unto himself. Therefore, in organized crime and in the Democratic Party, the standard-bearer of moral truths is nonexistent.

If you believe there is a purpose in this life you must believe in a higher power that wills that purpose. If you did not innately believe in that higher power, you would not be in search of that purpose. Like an animal, that purpose would be carnal instinct. The purpose would be pleasure and survival. Everything would begin and end there. No right and wrong. No morality. Only pleasure for the sake of pleasure: sex, drugs, leisure, revenge, gluttony, pride, greed, and atheism. Survival would be the only goal: abortion, murder, theft, violence, lawlessness, and exploitation are the result of such a mindset. If you are honest and take time to relegate the political Left and the Democratic Party to its lowest common denominators, you will encounter these vices not only present but also practiced in earnest.

The Mafia code of *omertà* is an old country code of silence, honor, and conduct from southern Italy. It is extraordinarily morally relative. Its practitioners are forbidden to cooperate with any government authority and operate outside of societal norms. The members are sworn to silence and make their living supplying society with "things" denied by the church and by the law.

Much of the rationale used by Mafia members to justify this lifestyle resembles that of the members of the Democratic Party. "I had no choice" is the most common refrain. Racism, poverty, single-parent families, bad role models, and no education are the most common excuses used to justify becoming a member of organized crime and the Democratic Party, but again, I repeat myself.

Moral relativism amongst the people must be cultivated. The ideology of the church, the Constitution, and moral capitalism cannot be allowed to be preached unchecked. My father would tell me: "You know what right and wrong is now, do what's right." For the Mafia, Triad, Crips, MS-13, Bloods, and Democratic Party to continue to thrive, children and society must be taught that there isn't any morality or right and wrong. They must be taught moral relativism.

Why is moral relativism bad for America? Founding Father Samuel Adams said,

> A general dissolution of principles and manners will more surely overthrow the liberties of America than the whole force of the common enemy. While the people are virtuous they cannot be subdued; but when once they lose their

virtue they will be ready to surrender their liberties to the first external or internal invader.

In the inner-city African American community, this "lack of
virtue" and moral relativism has become culturally ingrained. It
was created, cultivated, and sustained by the evil triumvirate of
organized crime, the political Left, and the Democratic Party.
For this reason, the values and politics of the Democratic Party
and organized crime are a great fit for the population of these
dystopias. The Democratic Party's values of blaming others, victimization, sloth, sexual immorality, and contempt for the law are
● identical to those of the street gang.

The Wikipedia page for the Crips street gang explained the
reasons for their genesis in this way:

> Gang activity in South Central Los Angeles
> has its roots in a variety of factors dating to the
> 1950s, including post-World War II economic
> decline leading to joblessness and poverty; racial
> segregation of young African American men,
> who were excluded from organizations such as
> the Boy Scouts, leading to the formation of black
> "street clubs"; and the waning of black national-
> ist organizations such as the Black Panther Party
> and the Black Power Movement.

What a load of crap!

Black people have always been poor. They've always been seg-
regated. They've always had challenges. But they didn't always kill
each other on an industrial level. What changed in the 1950s?
Marxism, through the Civil Rights Movement, had infiltrated
the black church and through it had infected every institution

with the fatal ideologies of victimization and sadistic government paternalism.

But the undercurrent of moral relativism is the tacit admission that your inferiority prevents you from competing in the legal world. Rather specifically, this inferiority exists because of education, family, poverty, or race. These ideas are reinforced ad nauseam to the point where you admit that you are inferior. Once you admit that damnable lie to yourself, you begin to act inferior, you seek out other inferiors as your peers, and you hate those that look like you.

One of the most amazing similarities between any organized crime syndicate and the Democratic Party is its members' penchant to harm and hate one another. Even though they are all evil and hateful, they seem to reserve their most extreme hate for people that look like them. The political Left and the Democratic Party are cannibalizing themselves. Like organized crime families, they have been led to kill each other on an industrial level. While Christian conservatives watch in horror, turf wars, petty disputes, chemical dependence, and pure hatred have led to a body count amongst them unmatched in the civilized world.

The hatred for fellow Italians during the Mafia wars throughout history has been notorious. We have all seen the pictures of bloody Italian mobsters in suits murdered by fellow Italians. The Organized Crime and Gang Section was designed to, among other things, sanction "hits" on fellow Italian mobsters.

The Godfather saga, *Goodfellas*, *Mobsters*, and *The Sopranos* all depicted and, in many ways, glorified this gratuitous violence and hatred toward their fellow Italians. These shows highlighted their cruelty, ignorance, and self-hatred. Like the political Left and Democrats, these criminals would include their wives and children in their crimes pressing them into their lifestyle. Power and greed are paramount. Innocent civilians are only collateral damage. This is their way.

Furthermore, the hatred taught to the Crips and Bloods by Soviet Marxists toward their fellow black Americans has led to wholesale fratricide and the formation of a police state wherever they reside. The outward evil and damage wrought by moral relativism are only possible when accompanied by an inner hatred of oneself. The production of self-hatred is the domain of the Democratic Party.

The Democrat-controlled neo-plantation and the Democrat-controlled public education system are very adroit at creating three things: self-hate, criminals, and Democrats. Some of the very elite manage to survive this indoctrination but they are a minority.

The political Left is controlled by "feelings." In religious terms, the political Left is controlled by the "flesh." Nothing is true. And when truth does not exist, everything is permitted.

This mindset is extraordinarily dangerous. For generations, organized crime and the Democratic Party have justified their immoral way of life. No rules. No compassion. Only one motivating factor: power. Acknowledging this danger in the hands of a few hundred mobsters can disrupt a big city. Consider its lethality in the realm of government. We've seen it in Nazi Germany, Communist China, and the USSR. But we saw it first among the slave-owning Democrats. It continues today.

Plato said, "The price of apathy towards public affairs is to be ruled by evil men." The roster of elected Democratic Party officials over the past 220 years elected by an apathetic populace has proven this to be true.

The religious standard of "thou shalt not kill" unless one is defending life, body, or property is an absolute for true Christians. Not so for those of the political Left. Like organized crime, with abortion, euthanasia, human trafficking, and the drug trade, they believe that they can kill for profit, for revenge, or just for plain annoyance.

Like organized crime, the political Left believes that it can: Steal, through over-taxation. Covet, by invoking income inequality, systemic racism, and white supremacy. They even believe in violating the First Commandment, "Thou shalt have no other God before me" by demanding that we obey the laws of government over those of God.

The political Left does not believe in observing the Sabbath, ensuring parental control of children, and not bearing false witness against their neighbor. The political Left believes in idol worship, taking God's name in vain, committing adultery, and every other sexual sin imaginable.

It can be said that the morality of organized crime and the political Left in the Democratic Party isn't relative. It is nonexistent. There has been a constant contest between the absolute morality of Christianity versus the moral relativism of the political Left and Christianity has always won.

In two thousand years, even though it has been consistently attacked, Christianity has never been defeated by evil empires. Christianity defeated them. Christianity defeated the Roman Empire, the transatlantic slave trade, the Confederacy, Nazism, and fascism, and it will defeat the Democratic Party.

The Democrats' moral relativism has led to an America that questions everything. This permissiveness and tolerance of all points of view has given the Democratic Party permission to not only question the existence of natural law but has provided them the arrogance to question biological realities and redefine them as they choose.

What is gender? The political Left, in its moral relativism, has successfully warped the already-immoral Democratic Party leadership to a point where it now has the temerity to ask this question. But it doesn't stop there. Democrats of authority and power are now demanding that people deny their religious convictions or lose scholarships, grants, investment dollars, and their livelihoods.

By attempting to coerce the American people into accepting the LGBTQ+ agenda in violation of their inalienable and constitutional rights to freedom of religion, the Democratic Party has become the most dangerous enemy the United States has ever faced. Niccolò Machiavelli wrote, "There is no surer sign of decay in a country than to see the rites of religion held in contempt."

The contempt that Democrats have for religion, specifically Christianity, is no longer theory or conjecture but absolute fact. As horrible as these actions may be, I have not yet disclosed the Democrats' most egregious treachery. Against the wishes of parents, Democrats are now commandeering the public education system as a tool to brainwash children against the values of their parents, into the morally relative, atheistic, and Marxist ideology of the Democratic Party. Because America's foundation is based on the freedom to practice one's religious beliefs without any coercion, if this transition becomes complete America will be lost forever.

Indeed, in the state of Florida, conservative governor Ron DeSantis discovered these illicit teachings in the educational curriculum of his state. The indoctrination of children into the atheist/Marxist/LGBTQ+ lifestyle had commenced in the public education system in Florida for children as early as five years old. Governor DeSantis immediately sought legislation outlawing this indoctrination. The Democrats and the LGBTQ+ community went crazy.

The Democrats called the bill the "Don't say gay" bill. And railed against it. But in their inane protest they revealed their real selves. They had to admit that they had in fact commandeered the public education system to groom and pimp children as sex objects to the LGBTQ+ community and that there is nothing wrong with it.

These same people now murder children in the womb until the time of birth and say there is nothing wrong with it. They castrate boys at the age of five and call them little girls and say there is nothing wrong with it. They are destroying the black community and saying there is nothing wrong with it.

The political Left will assist the Democratic Party in finishing what it started 160 years ago with the Confederacy and the Civil War. The Left will bankroll the Democrats' political takeover and assist them in turning America into an atheist/Marxist state where moral relativism will be written into law.

But not yet. The remnant has awakened. It is rising. While the high-water mark of the Democratic Confederacy is again at Gettysburg and has saddled up for "Pickett's charge," it will be turned back. And future generations will view this time in American history as they now view other times when Democrats possessed power over the American people and implemented slavery, the Confederacy, black codes, segregation, legalized murders, lawlessness, and insanity. They will view it as a time when the principles of freedom, justice, and morality again defeated the powers of darkness and held its defender in high esteem. This is the beginning of their end.

CHAPTER 10

♣

EXPLOITING A PATSY

*Nobody goes to jail. You know who
goes to jail, nigger stick up men.*
Henry Hill, *Goodfellas*

I n the miniseries *Queen*, written by Alex Haley, in the midst of
the Civil War, with the white men away fighting and fearing
the loss of her slaves, plantation mistress Sally Jackson, played
by Ann-Margret, resorted to a tactic that has always worked for
Democrats and organized crime to control the weak-minded.
She found a patsy. This time the patsy was the Union Army. One
night, around a bonfire, she gathered all of her slaves together
for a "talk"; male and female, field hands and house negros, black,
mulatto, quadroon, and octoroon. Standing amongst them,
unafraid, without any protection, Mistress Jackson said:

> Some of you have heard that this war is being
> fought for or against slavery. That is not true.
> The South is fighting for the right to protect its

own way of life. The alternative is too dreadful to imagine.

You've all heard of the stories of what happens to your people up North; hunger, sickness, poverty. This is not our way. When you are sick, we tend you. When you are hungry, we feed you. When you are old, we care for you.

And when you die, we bury you. That is our Christian duty.

Now I ask that you all kneel and pray with me.

Of course, the slaves fell for it. The weak-minded always fall for any explanation provided by those they perceive as superior. The patsy is another matter. A patsy is defined as a person who is easily taken advantage of, especially by being cheated or blamed for something. To be a patsy, one must be either unaware, uncaring, stupid, or an unethical accessory.

Before any great crime is committed, every great criminal mind will first find his patsy. Understanding that after the crime is discovered, the victim and the public will demand that someone pay, the master criminal must think ahead. Of course, receiving punishment is not part of the criminal's plan. Therefore, immediately after evolving his criminal conspiracy, the criminal's first task is to find a patsy.

Organized crime movies are replete with examples of criminal masterminds exploiting the patsy. In *The Godfather II*, Rocco Lampone was Michael Corleone's willing patsy in the murder of

Hyman Roth, and Frank Pentangeli was Hyman Roth's unwilling patsy in the betrayal of Michael Corleone.

In the above quote from the classic organized crime drama *Goodfellas*, Mafia member Henry Hill explains how the mob exploits black men as patsies. This disturbing yet revealing insight into organized crime management also highlights how much-organized crime and the Democratic Party have in common in their contempt for blacks.

The strategy of exploiting the unwilling patsy for political purposes is political Left politics 101. Jews were the scapegoats of the Nazis. Adolf Hitler blamed them for everything that went wrong in pre–World War II Germany. The Jewish people, not understanding the peril of the time, were caught unaware and were almost exterminated. Now the Jewish people say, "*Never again!*" Black Americans, the patsy for everything wrong in the Democratic Party, have never caught on. Consequently, their people are being exterminated right before our eyes as millions of patsies have been in the past.

Just as the leftist PLO continually exploit the Palestinians in the Middle East, the political Left and the Democratic Party exploit their own cultural suicide bombers here in America. The political Left is a death machine, and the Democratic Party is its assassin.

Either the criminals learned from the Democrats or Democrats from criminals, but one thing is for sure: They operate on a single-minded mission to obtain power.

Taking advantage of trusting people, the slave-owning Democratic Party elite made patsies of the Confederate soldiers during the Civil War and black Americans after it. And the political Left and Communists made patsies of the civil rights marchers during the Civil Rights Movement and make patsies of social justice marchers today.

Supposedly used by Stalin to describe the political Left in America, the term "useful idiots" is tailor-made for such people. The term refers to non-Communists who are regarded as susceptible to communist propaganda believing that it will lead to a democratic result. These "useful idiots," or patsies, continue in the vein of Black Lives Matter, Planned Parenthood, Antifa, the NEA, the NAACP, gun control advocates, and the National Action Network.

These patsies in their stupidity, ignorance, and hate will march, sweat, and advocate yearly to convince America to accept the tenants of Marxism, unaware that if successful, Marxism will lead to the end of the very freedoms that they used to advocate Marxism. Marxism will end freedom of religion, speech, assembly, press, and trial by jury. But the stupid patsy, which most of the black activists are, doesn't mind because he is so consumed with hate and envy that he doesn't know or care.

Democrats have taken this model as gospel. The unaware, uncaring, stupid, or accessory patsies are masterfully wielded by the political Left and their vehicle, the Democratic Party. The Republican Party, the National Rifle Association, teachers' unions, white Christians, Christianity, concerned parents, guns, police, traditional families, straight people, and the weather are just some of the issues that the Democrats tell the weak-minded are major threats, in order to deflect responsibility for Democratic Party theft, murder, and oppression.

The Democrats' most hapless and most utilized patsy, the Republican Party, some have said is an accessory. Staying true to a deal made with Democrats in 1992, if Democrats and Republicans voluntarily exclude themselves from each other's districts, Republicans would willingly remain silent and accept the blame for all the failings in the black community.

Democrats are allowed to accuse conservatives of the most horrible crimes. Conservatives who mostly employ the Republican Party as the vehicle to press their political agenda and defend their political honor are usually left defenseless as Democrats blame them for everything that is wrong with the black community. This is even more amazing when it is understood that Republicans represent zero majority-black areas and Democrats represent all of them.

The cryptic silence of the Republican Party while Democrats totally eviscerate the black community has led many to believe that Republicans do fall under the veneer of the willing or accessory patsy. Conservative policies like school choice, protection of life, defense of religious freedom, securing the border, defending the Second Amendment, and support of traditional families are very popular among black citizens. Black Americans might even vote for Republicans if Republicans spent a little time and money explaining these facts to them as opposed to being willing patsies for the Democratic Party when it comes to black oppression.

The gun, an inanimate object, could be an unwilling patsy of the Democratic Party. The insanity of this argument would be comical if it wasn't so troubling. The Joseph Goebbels line, "If you tell a lie big enough and keep repeating it, people will eventually come to believe it," is in full effect with respect to this argument.

Plato surmised that "human behavior flows from three main sources: desire, emotion, and knowledge." We all should strive to temper our behavior with knowledge rather than emotion or desire. Nevertheless, on the political Left the discussion over gun violence is enthralled with desire not knowledge on the side of the political professionals in the Democratic Party.

The knowledgeable Democratic operatives already know that there exists in any society a segment of the population where the emotion of desire can be manipulated to control every action. The desire to believe that the responsibility for one's safety can be transferred to a third party (the government) has been a foolish desire of the political Left since the Civil Rights Movement of the 1960s. Since their decisions with respect to this issue are driven by desire, no amount of information can change their minds. Therefore, it is easy for these patsies to be convinced that the gun is responsible for murder, not the individual. Democratic politicians exploiting these tragedies like ambulance-chasing attorneys activate these useful idiots in their scheme to persuade Americans to disarm themselves attaching their own chains.

There were 38,824 lives lost in traffic accidents in 2020; no one suggests banning cars. No one talked about banning planes after 9/11. No one talks about banning obesity after millions of heart attacks.

Why the attack on legal gun ownership? Because it is an impediment to everything that organized crime and the political Left seeks to do to the American people. An armed population can never be enslaved. An armed population cannot be oppressed, stripped of private property, raped, killed, or made to live in fear. America was never meant to be a police state.

The right to self-defense is an inalienable right. These rights are irrevocable, non-transferable, and unsellable. The goal, then, of organized crime and the Democratic Party is to convince the stupid patsy (the gun-control nuts, defund-the-police activists, and BLM supporters) that even though impossible, these rights can be sold and or transferred to the mob or to politicians. The results are always more crime, more dependence, more institutional breakdown, and more Democratic Party control. And the patsy always carries the burden while the true perpetrators incur the profit.

Two very willing patsies of the political Left and the Democratic Party are the Human Rights Campaign and the teachers' unions. The same public education or government education system that for decades has failed to educate our children now fails to protect them.

As I mentioned before and must reiterate, since the National Commission on Excellence in Education completed its report in 1983, it has been common knowledge that the government education system has been failing the vast majority of America's student population. However, failure is in the eyes of the beholder. For example, the failure of Nazi Germany was a success for America. Likewise, the failure of American parents and their children in the realm of education is a success for the political Left and the Democratic Party.

The report said, "The educational foundations of our society are presently being eroded by a rising tide of mediocrity that threatens our very future as a Nation and a people." It continued:

> Our once unchallenged pre-eminence in commerce, industry, science, and technology innovation is being overtaken by competitors throughout the world... If an unfriendly foreign power had attempted to impose on America the mediocre educational performance that exists today, we might well have viewed it as an act of war.

That was forty years ago, and the system has gotten worse. Nevertheless, the United States still spends more money on education than any other country in the world. This is a plan. It is intentional.

The Democratic Party understands that it would be political suicide for the American people to discover that the Democrats have commandeered the public education system established by parents and financed to educate their children to reflect their values and have turned it into an instrument of their destruction. Therefore, they need a patsy. The National Education Association and the American Federation of Teachers have both volunteered.

Knowing that the public has no control and cannot un-elect their leadership, Democrats routinely allow the teachers' unions, the NEA, and the ATF to take the blame for the failure of public education. For the continuation of their monopoly and yearly increases in educational spending the unions gladly accept the blame. Movies such as *Lean On Me, Won't Back Down, Hard Times at Douglass High*, and *Waiting for Superman* addressed the terrible conditions of the public education system. These movies mentioned the politicians, the unions, the parents, and the students but never mentioned the main culprit: the Democratic Party.

Another willing patsy of the Democratic Party is the political arm of the anti-Christian movement that goes by the benign name of the Human Rights Campaign. The Human Rights Campaign claims to advocate for the rights of the LGBTQ+ community. It does not. The Human Rights Campaign cares less for the LGBTQ+ community than the NAACP cares about the black community. The Human Rights Campaign wields the psychological pain and need for acceptance by the LGBTQ+ community as a means to an end. That end is atheism in America.

The belief in atheism is a necessity for the terror and mental subjugation needed for the desired totalitarian state of the

Democratic Party. The concepts of inalienable rights and a higher law than man's law is an anathema to the tyrant.

This attitude was on full display on June 2, 2022, when *The Washington Times* reported that black and openly gay New York Democrat Representative Mondaire Jones, while sitting on the House Judiciary Committee, declared:

> Enough of your thoughts and prayers. Enough. You will not stop us from advancing the "Protecting Our Kids Act" today. You will not stop us from passing it in the House next week, and you will not stop us there. If the filibuster obstructs us, we will abolish it. If the Supreme Court objects, we will expand it. And we will not rest until we have taken weapons of war out of circulation in our communities.

Actions taken by the political Left are never viewed through a moral prism. Like the sexual actions of all unmarried people, in traditional Christianity and other religions the LGBTQ+ "lifestyle" is considered sinful, and if one participates in it one must repent. Most LGBTQ+ Christians adhered to this admonition until the Human Rights Campaign began to advocate "pride."

Pride, one of the seven deadly sins and seven vices, is opposite to its virtue, which is humility. There is nothing humble with respect to organized crime, the political Left, or the Democratic Party. All three are seething with pride. The Democratic Party and the Human Rights Campaign have even deemed June "LGBTQ+ Pride Month." Democrats cunningly forget to mention to all their adherents that to accept the Democratic Party concept of LGBTQ+ pride one must reject true Christianity. Democrats have therefore established a type of apostate "Christianity du jour," where, like "gender fluidity," one can practice a different Christianity daily.

The Democrats understand that their party cannot openly advocate the end of Christianity. But they can advocate the normalization of LGBTQ+ pride and lifestyle, thus acquiring atheism by default while blaming their willing patsy, the Human Rights Campaign, and the LGBTQ+ community when the proverbial crap hits the fan.

In a June 4, 2020, *Washington Post* article titled "How schools are learning to teach gender identity," the Human Rights Campaign, "LGBTQ," and "conservative" were mentioned many times. But the vehicle employed to implement these sadistic grooming mechanisms into law—the Democratic Party—was not mentioned once.

Every crime organization needs patsies. As you see, the political Left and Democrats already have theirs lined up with bullseyes taped to their chests.

CHAPTER 11

FALSE PIETY

> Priest: *Michael Francis Rizzi,*
> *do you renounce Satan?*
> Michael Corleone: *I do renounce him.*
> Priest: *And all of his works?*
> Michael Corleone: *I do renounce them.*
> Priest: *And all of his pomps?*
> Michael Corleone: *I do renounce them.*
> Priest: *Michael Rizzi, will you be baptized?*
> Michael Corleone: *I will.*
> Priest: *Michael Rizzi, go in peace.*
> Baptism scene, *The Godfather*

T he accouterments of the Catholic Church are a staple in the Mafia. They disguise their true intentions of violence, power, and greed by cloaking them in the love and peace of Jesus Christ. Shamefully, these tactics have been incorporated by the political Left and the Democratic Party. I take no pleasure in saying that this false piety is so much a part of the black church that the two are almost synonymous. The Catholic Church has finally concluded that politicians in the Democratic Party are eviler than the Mafia, and the church is finally starting to respond.

Even though, as evil as they are, members of La Cosa Nostra or the Mafia have never been denied Communion. Maybe they've never refused to confess their sins or seek forgiveness.

Nevertheless, the arrogance, pride, and evil of the Democratic Party have become so great that they now give orders to God. The First Commandment, "Thou shalt have no other gods before me," has no effect on the Democratic Party. In their minds, the Democratic Party leadership is God. After numerous warnings from the Catholic Church that their stance on abortion and LGBTQ+ policies are against the Word of God, on October 27, 2019, Father Robert Morey, the pastor at Saint Anthony Catholic Church in Florence, South Carolina, denied Communion to Joe Biden. On October 29, 2021, the *New York Times* reported, "The nation's Roman Catholic bishops in June advanced a conservative push to deny communion to President Biden, the nation's second Catholic president."

And on May 25, 2022, CBS News reported that because of her stance on abortion and her refusal to repent or seek forgiveness, Speaker of the House Nancy Pelosi was also denied Communion by the Catholic archbishop of San Francisco. It must be noted these denials of Communion commenced only after many warnings were given to and rebuffed by Biden and Pelosi. Ergo, Biden and Pelosi have effectively said that they are God. Thus, fulfilling the prophecy of the "Son of Perdition" in 2 Thessalonians 2:3–4:

> Let no one deceive you by any means: for that
> Day will not come, unless the falling away comes
> first, and the man of sin is revealed, the son of

perdition who opposeth and exalteth himself
above all that is called God or that is worshipped;
so that he as God sitteth in the temple of God,
shewing himself that he is God.

But this attitude isn't new for the political Left. It is a job
requirement.

Like organized crime syndicates, Democrats redefine the rules
of God as they see fit. Based on their standards, the Mafia, Crips,
Bloods, and Triad decide who lives and who dies. They decide
what is right and what is wrong. They take what they want from
those who earn and distribute it to whomever they please. As a
law unto themselves, they rape, pillage, and burn as they please.

Sitting in the seat of God, the political Left and the Democratic
Party led by Joe Biden, Jim Clyburn, and Nancy Pelosi are no different. They have decided to proclaim the laws and creations of
nature as null and void. God defined marriage as a union between
a man and a woman. They have redefined marriage from a union
between one man and one woman to a union between two men,
two women, two women and one man, two men and one woman,
or anything anyone says it is. Which means that marriage, to
them, is nothing.

Nature created men and women distinctively differently.
Science had observed this creation and concluded that men were
defined as anyone with XY chromosomes, and women as anyone with XX chromosomes. The political Left and their minions
in the Democratic Party on their own authority have redefined
nature's creation and natural law. There is now no definition of
man or woman. In addition, all must accept this lie and partake in
it or be punished.

After the murder of George Floyd, the Left sent out its "brown shirts" in the form of BLM and Antifa and like organized crime, demanded the defunding of police and the disarming of citizens while its adherents systematically burned, pillaged, and murdered their way to power.

The so-called protector of the commands of God, the black preacher, has mostly joined his Democratic masters in full-throated support for this violent assault on biblical teachings, the church, and natural law itself. It should be expected. The black church was compromised in the early 1960s via the Civil Rights Movement. As discussed, after many warnings from the bishops, the false piety of the Rev. Dr. Martin Luther King, Jr. was revealed, leading to his excommunication from the black Baptist church in 1961. He did not change his ways. He started the Progressive National Baptist Convention and continued in his partnership with the Marxist political Left. In this partnership, King led black Americans away from the salvation of Jesus Christ and into the clutches of government dependence, victimization, envy, self-hatred, and death. He led the transformation of the black church into a mostly impotent, apostate church and a vassal of the racist and Marxist Democratic Party.

In the HBO series *The Wire*, among other things, it was revealed that many black preachers prostitute their churches as money launderers for the local drug dealers in their communities. This explanation can go a long way in explaining why so many young black people are rejecting the teachings of the church and why their lands are left desolate.

The political Left and the Democratic Party have mastered this false piety. In *The Prince*, the bible of immoral hardball politics and a book that every politician has read, Niccolò Machiavelli warned against the undermining of religion. In more than one chapter he wrote about it. He said, "There is nothing more important than appearing to be religious."

Machiavelli also wrote, "There is no surer sign of decay in a country than to see the rites of religion held in contempt." But if there is any doubt that the Democrats understand that their attack on religion will eventually destroy this country, read this admonition from their hero and teacher Machiavelli:

> And as observance of religious teachings is the cause of the greatness of republics, similarly, disdain for it is the cause of their ruin. For where the fear of God is lacking, the state must necessarily either come to ruin or be held together by the fear of a prince that will compensate for the lack of religion.

The Democratic Party leadership has taken this mantra to heart. Its members want a strong prince or government. They know that the destruction of religion is the only way to create their all-powerful prince or government. Machiavelli has given them the playbook and they have mastered it. They are evil and have bamboozled generations of Americans of every race.

Earlier I explained how the near destruction of an already-compromised black church occurred at the hands of Rev. Dr. Martin Luther King, Jr. and the Marxists/Communists of the political Left in the Civil Rights Movement. But how did the political Left graft itself into the foundation of the white Protestant church and the Catholic Church? And how is false piety allowed to continue unabated and mostly unchallenged? Greed.

Greed is one of the seven vices whose opposite is the virtue of charity. Volumes and volumes can be and have been written with respect to the greed in the Catholic Church. This greed led to the ultimate break up of that ancient institution. The Catholic Church's selling of indulgences and Martin Luther's 1517 letter of complaint to Bishop Albrecht von Brandenburg precipitated a chain of events that would eventually commence the Protestant revolution.

The pope and the priests claimed that the purchase of one of these indulgences would release a named loved one's soul from purgatory, sending the soul to heaven. Catholic priest Martin Luther, knowing this was untrue, "protested" these lies along with others. The Catholic Church's persistence caused Martin Luther and his followers, the "Protestants," to break away, forming their own religious denomination.

The greed remains in much of the Catholic Church, with organized crime and leftist Catholic politicians exploiting this greed by purchasing their fake piety. The Protestant church isn't any better.

In America, greed generated from the institution of slavery created an apostate religious system in the South, justifying a belief in white supremacy and black inferiority among both races. This apostate religion still exists in the members of both races who remain true to the Democratic Party. But even while the vast majority of Southern, mostly white Protestant religious congregations have formally rejected the previous racism of their churches and ancestors, most black Protestant churches, I can say with some degree of certainty, are led by some of the most ignorant racists in America who teach the apostate religious doctrine of black liberation theology.

Many of these "preachers" are infected with the co-vanities of pride and greed. Politicians and every other crook reside in their sanctuaries not to take advantage of the church's offer of love, forgiveness, and reconciliation. They are there to take advantage of the preacher's offer to assist them in maintaining the lie.

The ideology and fake piety of the sellout Democratic black preacher is vividly displayed by Tucker Carlson in his book *The Long Slide*. In it, Carlson recalls a conversation with "Reverend" Al Sharpton:

> What does Al Sharpton want? He didn't even pause when I asked. "What we want is them." By them Sharpton means every white liberal in the leadership of the Democratic Party who has ever assumed a high-handed tone with him, put him off for a meeting, or in any way acted supercilious or superior in his presence.
>
> That's a lot of people. Sharpton says he'll start by demanding control over the party. From there, he'd like a hand in picking next year's vice presidential nominee.
>
> After that, we'll see… In the end, of course, Sharpton isn't really running for president of the United States.
>
> He's running for president of black America.

About Jesse Jackson, Carlson records Sharpton as saying:

> They got Jackson little by little, Sharpton believes,
> mostly by giving him things, money jobs for his
> friends, the use of private airplanes. Within a year
> or two, Jackson was an employee. Sharpton con-
> siders it a profound political lesson. "I saw what
> happened to Jesse. I was there. They're assuming I
> want what Jesse wanted."

Reviewing this conversation, when asked what he wanted,
Al Sharpton said nothing about bringing more people to Christ,
joining the church, getting baptized, or calls to repentance. These
ecclesiastical matters that should mean everything to a true man
of God actually mean nothing to him. In fact, they were never
even mentioned. Sharpton, being a sellout apostate when asked
what he wanted, only spoke of politics. In my opinion and based
on the description in Matthew 7:15–20, he is a false prophet.

The condition of the black community reveals them as false.
Therefore, their piety is false.

In his conversation with Sharpton, Tucker Carlson reveals
the mentality of the offspring of the Rev. Dr. Martin Luther King
Jr. and the Civil Rights Movement: the Democratic Party's apostate black preachers. These men view the church as nothing more
than a stepping stone to money, women, and political power. The
dysfunction in the black community is directly correlated to the
moral relativity and apostasy of the Democratic black preacher.
The dysfunction in America is directly correlated to the moral
relativity of the political Left and the Democratic Party modeled
by their mentor in organized crime.

CHAPTER 12

♣

PRIDE

Tom: *You've won. Do you
wanna wipe everyone out?*
Michael: *I don't feel I have to wipe
out everyone. Just my enemies.*
The Godfather II

he above statement from *The Godfather II* highlights Michael
Corleone's pride. His pride led to the destruction of his business, his family, and himself. Proverbs 16:18 says, "Pride
goeth before destruction." Members of organized crime are consumed with the sin and the crime of pride. It drives their wicked
ambition and their avarice.

In *Mere Christianity*, C. S. Lewis said this about pride:

> There is one vice of which no man in the world
> is free; which everyone in the world loathes when
> he sees it in someone else and of which hardly
> any people, except Christians, ever imagine that

they are guilty themselves... There is no fault which makes a man more unpopular, and no fault which we are more unconscious of in ourselves. And the more we have it ourselves, the more we dislike it in others... The vice I am talking about is Pride or Self-Conceit: and the virtue opposite to it, in Christian morals, is called Humility.

According to Christian teachers, the essential vice, the utmost evil, is Pride. Unchastity, anger, greed, and all that are mere fleabites in comparison: it was through Pride that the devil became the devil: Pride leads to every other vice: It is the complete anti-God state of mind.

It is interesting that in 1952, when C. S. Lewis wrote these words, he could not have comprehended that in the future, something as evil as the political Left could exist in a civilized society. He wrote of pride, "hardly any people except Christians ever imagine that they are guilty themselves...no fault which we are more unconscious of in ourselves."

Even though they are completely anti-Christian, this is not true for the political Left. They have not only admitted to the sin of pride but completely embrace it, encourage it, and promote it as a lifestyle choice. Even the Mafia and the Triad have not been so brazen. Even though warnings from the Bible and scholars from antiquity have warned against it, calling pride a "deadly sin." Gay pride, black pride, LGBTQ pride, abortion pride, feminist pride, and other destructive forms of pride flourish on the political Left, turning it into a death cult.

The word *humility*, the opposite of pride, is never taken seriously by the Left. Being offensive, uncharitable, ill-mannered, disrespectful, and shocking is their portion. Christians, unlike the Left, should be loath to offend. Nevertheless, we are not allowed to lie. Therefore, if the truth offends, be offended. Offending for the sake of Christ and the truth is the only time we, as Christians, are allowed to offend.

Acknowledging that a humble spirit is required for one to be an apt pupil. The Left infects our children with this deadly sin of pride, rendering them unteachable. Their constant demand for more free stuff, government action against their enemies, and government-mandated acceptance and promotion of their immoral behavior illustrate their pride and contempt for all that is good and right.

Organized crime is no different. Like the Left, it cares nothing for the condition of the communities it ravages. Street gangs routinely spray bullets into crowds of people, killing innocents, including children and the elderly. According to Gun Violence Archive, 999 children, ages under one to eleven, were killed with guns in 2020, and 4,142 children, ages twelve to seventeen, were killed with guns that same year.

Murder, drugs, theft, sexual perversion, hate, and vengeance—all crimes whose genesis rests in the bosom of pride.

"No justice, no peace!" Revenge! Envy! Greed! These maladies fuel organized crime and the Democratic Party.

CHAPTER 13

♣

EXPLOIT THE WEAK,
ENCOURAGE VICE

*We have the gambling and the unions
and they are the best things to have, but
narcotics is the thing of the future.*
Tom Hagen, *The Godfather*

The weak and the vulnerable are not helped by hyenas and vultures; they are devoured. Organized crime has a special talent for eyeing the abused, the fearful, and the abandoned and preying on them. The above statement from the movie *The Godfather* features Mafia lawyer Tom Hagen explaining to the boss Vito Corleone why it was pertinent for the family to expand into another realm of exploitation: the drug trade.

It is pure opportunism. Another way for criminals to make money from the misery of others. It is the way of the decrepit coward. Devoid of honor or virtue, this is now the domain of the political Left in the Democratic Party.

For its entire existence, the exploitation of the weak and vulnerable has been the schtick of the Democratic Party. In the past, they exploited black slaves, poor whites, freedmen, and Catholics. Today their exploitation has become more nuanced. The evolution of the law has rendered it almost impossible for Democrats to exploit Americans solely on account of race. Once, under the vise of the Ku Klux Klan, the Democrats could prowl the city streets and back roads of America, killing whomever they chose without fear of legal retribution because of corruption, and without fear of moral retribution because of black male cowardice. Those days are over. In an act of pure political genius, Democrats have concocted ways to lure their prey legally.

By passing a series of negative laws pertaining to gambling, LGBTQ+ rights, safe injection sites, gender fluidity, abortion, drug legalization, no bail, and gun control, they have decided to exploit, not help, the people suffering from these disorders and addictions.

To demoralize an entire American population, as they have most blacks from slavery till now, is the Democrats' primary goal. Like organized crime, it is their model. To make them quit and render them hopeless is their aim. In *The Old Man and the Sea*, Ernest Hemingway wrote, "It's easy when you're beat." I have seen beaten people. Devoid of hope. No plans for the future. Believing that the government decides their worth. It is an undead life. And the Democrats wish it upon all of us.

They intentionally inflict pain. The pain is the point. You can never be allowed to come to any conclusion by your own counsel. Thinking for oneself leads to freedom. Your decisions must originate from a place of fear—from a place of dread. In this place of shadows and darkness dwell organized crime and the Democratic Party.

If you are a drug addict, like the Mafia, in order to exploit your addiction, not cure it, the Democrats intend to build safe injection sites all over the country. These safe injection sites are just Democrat-supported, federally funded crack houses. Criminals cannot make money from a dead addict. And it is harder, although not impossible, for criminal Democrats to retrieve a vote from a dead voter. The goal is to keep the addict alive and using while also voting for his pusher, the Democratic Party. Indeed, on March 9, 2022, the Associated Press reported on a safe injection site in Democrat-controlled New York City:

> Equipped and staffed to reverse overdoses, New York City's new, privately run "overdose prevention centers" are a bold and contested response to a storm tide of opioid overdose deaths nationwide… Supporters say the sites—also known as safe injection sites or supervised consumption spaces—are humane, realistic responses to the deadliest crisis in U.S. history. Critics see them as illegal and defeatist answers to the harm that drugs wreak on users and communities.

As I've said before, there has never been a time in American history when Democrats have not demanded a way to murder Americans legally. I have written at length about how Democrats exploit the fear and shame of young women to lure them to death houses or abortion clinics strategically positioned in places to ensure that they eradicate that part of the citizenry they consider unworthy of life.

Usafacts.org reports that Democrats have finagled $1.29 billion in total government funding, $553.7 million federal, for Planned Parenthood to carry out their murderous procedures.

Anyone that cares for women should wish that they never suffer an abortion. Nevertheless, the political Left has developed a society where pornography, a complete lack of morals, and the sexual grooming of children go hand in hand with a burgeoning abortion, transgender, and pharmaceutical industry getting rich on Obamacare money.

Why would Democrats promote laws that would destroy America? Two reasons: They are evil, and they get paid. On August 26, 2014, a *Daily Beast* headline reads, "Obamacare Now Pays for Gender Reassignment." Sex reassignment surgery is now an industry. Doctors are paid for every child they castrate and mutilate. A doctor who will abort a child definitely has no problem castrating one. These doctors are also paid for a lifetime supply of drugs and puberty blockers forced on children as young as five by mentally ill, abusive, or brainwashed parents.

Indeed, on September 26, 2022, Matt Walsh reported on his show that Vanderbilt University Hospital medical director Dr. Shane Taylor said she encouraged the university to start conducting transgender surgeries because they are "big money makers." She reiterated that phalloplasty surgery (creating a fake penis) could be worth up to $100,000. After Republican Governor Bill Lee called for an investigation and conservative backlash ensued in the red state of Tennessee, Vanderbilt backed down. Nevertheless, other hospitals are going full speed ahead. Again, like organized crime, you find the Democratic Party exploiting the mentally disturbed, the weak, and children for profit. The transgender funding in Democratic Party–supported Obamacare makes all of this possible.

Because of the censorship from the five families, it is difficult for average Americans to counter them. Difficult, not impossible.

About gender dysphoria, the Mayo Clinic says, "A diagnosis for gender dysphoria is included in the *Diagnostic and Statistical Manual of Mental Disorders* (DSM-V), a manual published by the American Psychiatric Association. The diagnosis was created to help people with gender dysphoria get access to necessary health."

Americans suffering from gender dysphoria are children of God and citizens. They should not be maligned, persecuted, or mistreated. They should be helped. The same is said for any member of the LGBTQ+ community, except those who choose to force their lifestyles on others. But Democrats and the political Left do not help; like all criminals, they only exploit. They never call you to greatness or repentance. They want you to be comfortable in your weakness.

Prayer, counseling, truth, and self-control are required to deal with sexual immorality. The most important of all of them is self-control. Self-control is one of the Fruits of the Spirit written about in Galatians 5:22–23. The others are love, joy, peace, patience, kindness, and generosity. Not believing in the Holy Spirit, the political Left possesses none of these characteristics and, therefore, can only accept and exploit these maladies but never deliver the afflicted.

Unless one is mentally ill, all behavior can be learned and unlearned. Many of these Americans are mentally ill. However, the acceptance and promotion of mentally ill behavior can groom people who are not suffering from these afflictions to voluntarily assume the behavior for various reasons. Nazism, fascism, Communism, the Confederacy, and the Democratic Party are the result of evil or insane people commandeering the levers of government, thus camouflaging their insane behavior with the legitimate veneer of law, turning once-moral nations into a mob of psychopaths. This mass insanity produced dysfunctional societies in

Germany, Italy, Russia, and Eastern Europe, inevitably leading to the suicide of a nation. This is now happening in America on an epidemic level. If not stopped, as with the aforementioned nation states, the suicide of this nation will be the inevitable result of this state-sanctioned insanity.

I consider the laws protecting these actions and promoting them as death laws. Promoting such laws ensures an expansion of this destructive behavior. Since this behavior cannot produce children, it will logically end in the depopulation and destruction of America.

Like organized crime, the Left seeks a nation where evil is not only accepted but where it will prosper. Nevertheless, evil always fails. It fails because the twin prizes sought, power and destruction, cannot coexist. To have a functioning society, you must have order. You cannot have order in a state of constant destruction.

So, while the Left promotes the murder of their own children and the death of their constituents through drug abuse, while the Left promotes the infertility of its own base and the promotion of vice, we conservative Christians will continue living as God commanded.

Normal people will have children, not abort them. We will love our children, not exploit them. We will discipline our children, not sexually groom them. We will practice self-control and not give in to the addiction of drug abuse. We will work and earn and never beg. We will protect our possessions, our families, and ourselves without permission from any government. We are, and will remain, *free*.

CHAPTER 14

♣

CONSPIRACY

*I want you to arrange a meeting
with the five families.*
Vito Corleone, *The Godfather*

T rayvon Martin got killed stopping to get Skittles: A lie. Michael Brown, "Hands up, don't shoot!" A lie. George Floyd: White police are systematically executing black men. A lie. Freddie Gray: Police beat him to death in the back of their van. Another lie.

All of these lies resulted in riots, billions of dollars in property damage, and dozens of lives lost. How did the lie get loose? Conspiracy. Criminal conspiracy, simply put, is an agreement to commit an unlawful act.

In the above quotation from *The Godfather*, to organize the drug trade in New York City, Vito Corleone instructs his mob lawyer Tom Hagen to call five Mafia crime families to a meeting. This is a classic conspiracy. An agreement to commit a criminal act.

A criminal conspiracy exists among the five crime families of New York, just as a criminal conspiracy exists among the five crime families of the political Left: the media, civil rights organizations, academia, big tech, and the Democratic Party. The above-mentioned racial lies could have become accepted as fact only if these sources colluded in spreading this false information.

The political Left is so consumed with evil and fear that it's even attempted to censor speeches of foreign leaders that do not measure up to their twisted standards. A lie is never censored. It is not dangerous. The truth, however, can bring down nations. As Thomas Sowell observed, "It's amazing how much panic one honest man can spread among a multitude of hypocrites."

Indeed, on September 28, 2022, Caroline Downey reported in *National Review*, "YouTube Removes Incoming Italian Prime Minister Meloni's Passionate Speech on Family Breakdown." To the absolute horror of the political Left, far-right candidate Giorgia Meloni was elected prime minister of Italy. Immediately, the five families of the political Left soon conspired to paint her as a fascist, censoring her from the American public.

Maintaining its part in the conspiracy, claiming that the speech violated YouTube's Community Guidelines, YouTube censored a speech by Meloni. What was so egregious about Meloni's speech? According to Downy, Meloni said it's scandalous for people to defend the natural family founded on marriage, to want to increase the birth rate, to want to place the correct value on human life, to support freedom in education, and to say no to gender ideology. She repudiated the accusations that the World Congress of Families represents a step backward for Italy, saying leftists, whom she said protested and tried to censor the event, are the regressive ones. Meloni slammed surrogacy which she called "degrading and abusive of women," late-term abortion, and child gender transition hormone therapy. She called the low birth rate one of the "biggest problems facing Europe." The embarrassing ones are those who support practices like "womb for rent" abortion at nine months and blocking the development of children with drugs at eleven years of age, she said.

These words of common sense, morality, and right behavior caused a criminal conspiracy among the five families of the political Left to plan her censor here in America.

After an outcry from conservatives, YouTube lifted the ban.

Conspiring to indoctrinate and groom Christian children into the LGBTQ+ lifestyle without the knowledge and against the wishes of their parents is another conspiracy propagated by this five-headed hydra. The many groups that hate America, like NAMBLA and the Human Rights Campaign, Facebook and Twitter, public schools and universities, Black Lives Matter, the NAACP, and the Democratic Party, are all working together. They have two goals: power and chaos.

Their aim is to cause harm. Their cause is immoral. Their cause is evil. Because it is evil and there is an agreement to assist each other in the furtherance of these actions, their actions are just as much a criminal conspiracy as those conducted by the five families of the Mafia.

These five families of the political Left conspired to censor and punish any American who spoke out against the COVID-19 crackdown. They conspired to censor and punish anyone who spoke ill of the election of Joe Biden. They conspired to censor any information critical of the Hunter Biden laptop. They conspire to censor and punish anyone who speaks against the LGBTQ+ agenda, for gun rights, or mentions the name of Jesus Christ.

Greg Piper highlighted this conspiracy in an October 1, 2022, piece for *Just the News* titled, "Enemies list? Fed-backed censorship machine targeted 20 news sites." He wrote,

> The private consortium that reported election "misinformation" to big tech platforms during the 2020 election season, in "consultation" with federal agencies, targeted several news organizations in its dragnet... Websites for Just the News, New York Post, Fox News, Washington Examiner, Washington Times, Epoch Times, and Breitbart were identified among the 20 "most prominent domains across election integrity incidents" that were cited in tweets flagged by the election Integrity Partnership and its collaborators." No news organizations should be subjected to an enemies/censorship list for reporting newsworthy facts," Just the News Editor in Chief, John Solomon said in a statement. "It's even more egregious that this censorship machinery was prodded, aided and sanctioned by the federal government.

There isn't any shame in organizing. I wish average Americans were as proficient as the political Left in this arena. But when one decides to organize for an immoral and evil purpose, you are now involved in a criminal conspiracy.

Organizing these types of conspiracies will put an entire nation in peril. For you that applauded when the five families of the Left censored those who questioned Joe Biden's election or when the FBI raided President Donald Trump's private residence at Mar-a-Lago and the many coordinated state and federal investigations aimed at him, the great American patriot Thomas Paine wrote, "He that would make his own liberty secure must guard even his enemy from oppression; for if he violates this duty, he establishes a precedent that will reach himself."

Intimidation and violence have been a part of the Left's political playlist since the Democratic Party's inception in 1800. The plantation overseers, the Confederate army, the Ku Klux Klan, the civil rights organizations, Black Lives Matter, and Antifa—these criminal organizations have been the violent military wing of the Democratic Party over the past two centuries.

Although very seldom prosecuted, the violence created by these groups for the Left and the Democratic Party is illegal, immoral, and therefore criminal.

The Constitution of the United States guarantees every state a republican form of government. A republican form of government is a government where the power is held by the people. The people lend power to public servants they elect to represent them and serve their interests. How can a republican form of government exist when, due to fear, bribery, or malfeasance, citizens are disenfranchised?

The FBI search of Mar-a-Lago, President Donald Trump's Florida residence, was one of the latest attempts in the Left's two-century-long attempt to enslave the citizens of the United States of America. However, this violation is unprecedented. The Left is actively probing the American citizenry. It determines how much disrespect and tyranny we are willing to accept from our government. It will dole out whatever we accept. For, if this can be done to a former president without pushback from the people, none of us is safe.

Evil does not sleep. Every nation that has ever allowed evil organizations to conspire to systematically break the laws of man and nature has lived to regret it. It did not take long for the entire nation to be consumed in fire and death. The Democratic Party and the political Left today celebrate their ability to do something we thought was impossible in America. They have the ability to stifle free speech, control the media, sexually groom children, intimidate political opposition, confiscate private property, coerce drug injections, and close businesses.

All tyrannies start by convincing a begrudged subsection of the people that if they give the government power, the government will use that power to punish their enemies. Hitler did this with the Jews. Lenin used this with the bourgeoisie. And Mao had the capitalists. The prosecution of Donald Trump, anyone who believes in the Trump message of "Make America Great Again" (MAGA), Christians, and conservatives by the political Left are red meat for tyrannical Democrat leadership. Goodreads.com quotes Aldous Huxley,

> The surest way to work up a crusade in favor of some good cause is to promise people they will have a chance of maltreating someone. To be able to destroy with good conscience, to be able to behave badly and call your bad behavior "righteous indignation"—this is the height of psychological luxury, the most delicious of moral treats.

For those who applaud the illegal persecution of your enemies today: Rest assured, they will soon come for you.

We must be strong. We must be brave. The slave is weak, a coward, and unhappy. Being weak and a coward, he refuses to exercise his freedom, blaming others for his condition. He flails about, protesting, rioting, and looting. Not understanding that he is the cause and solution to all of his problems. Remember, the first rule of self-love is never to allow abuse to yourself, especially self-inflicted. The slave fails at enforcing this rule every second he remains part of the Marxist political Left and the Democratic Party.

There are still free people in this country. How do I know? Because America still stands. Our national anthem, "The Star-Spangled Banner," ends by calling America the land of the free and the home of the brave. It is poignant and fitting. Aristotle said, "You will never do anything in this world without courage. It is the greatest quality of the mind next to honor." One must be brave to be free.

There can be no happiness without freedom, and there can be no freedom without courage. There can be no courage without strength. Therefore, before it is possible for us to exercise our freedom, we must first be strong and brave. There are still those in America who are strong enough to exercise their freedom. We do not ask for a respite from our adversary. We welcome the fight! We do not beg. We earn. We do not ask anyone to give us our freedom. We defy our adversaries to try to take it.

EPILOGUE

♣

MY FATHER'S GLASS DOOR

Michael, you are blind.
It wasn't a miscarriage. It was an
abortion. An abortion Michael.
Something that is unholy and evil.
Like our marriage is an abortion.
Something unholy and evil.
Kay Corleone, *The Godfather II*

When you wed yourself to something that is evil, it tends to have an evil and corrupting influence. It will destroy you, or you must destroy it. If you are to survive, you must abort the evil relationship. This hard lesson is revealed in a childhood memory of mine. The memory of my father and his glass door.

My father was born in the Democratic Party–controlled Jim Crow South toward the end of the Great Depression and in the midst of World War II. He was abandoned by both parents at six weeks old and raised on a plantation by his great-aunt and -uncle, who were kind and God-fearing but were victims of the area where they lived. Like today, Democrats hated black Americans and proclaimed that they would either obey or die. Thus, my ancestors were poor and not well educated. They were expected to stay in their place and teach their children the same.

In this environment, my father was expected to merely survive, not thrive. He was taught to plow a mule at the age of eight and was put to work, as he said, from "can't see morning to can't see night." He was expected to do this for the rest of his life. Most of his peers and contemporaries had succumbed and conformed to this expected life of poverty, hard labor, and abuse at the hands of their more-than-two-century masters in the Democratic Party. But not all.

Carl Jung said, "I am not what happened to me. I am what I choose to become." As a testimony to Jung's beliefs, sometimes, a flower will burst through the concrete to bask in the glory of the sun. My father was one such flower.

In 1965, the white Democrat plantation owner summoned my father for the annual fraud fest called "settling up time." Like organized crime, the plantation system of the Democrat-controlled South was an extortion and loan-sharking racket with the corruption of government officials as a side deal. My father had been a victim of this system all of his life. The white Democrat plantation owner would loan the black sharecropper money either through cash or credit. The owner would also provide a shack and all materials for planting and harvesting for the year.

At the end of the year, after receiving all the money from the harvest and deducting expenses, the white Democrat plantation owner and the black sharecropper would, in theory, divide the proceeds fifty/fifty. This meeting was called "settling up time." Like a Mafia extortion and loan-shark scheme, the white Democrat plantation owner always extorted the illiterate and fearful black plantation owner by telling him that after extracting all expenses, the profits were non-existent, and the sharecropper actually owed *him*. If the sharecropper protested, the plantation owner would remind him that the sheriff and the courts would always take the side of the white Democrat and that the black sharecropper had three choices: pay the debt, continue to work for him, or go to jail.

My father demanded that the plantation owner write down exactly what he owned under his signature. Somehow he paid the owed amount. And left that life forever.

After aborting his relationship with the plantation system and the real bigotry of low expectations, my father procured a job working at a lumber mill. He didn't earn much money but was free from the cotton fields. We lived like most black and white people in the poverty-ridden, racist, and ill-educated Democrat-controlled Jim Crow South. Our four-room, rented, asphalt shingle-sided home had no running water, wood heat, and a tin roof, but there was a covered screened back porch.

One cold night coming home from work, my father arrived in his truck. I was around four years old. He called me outside, which was uncustomary at night. He said he needed my help carrying something as I hurried outside. I noticed he had a large cardboard box lying in the back of his truck. It was heavy, so heavy that he needed my help carrying it into the house.

When I asked what was in the box, he explained that it was a "sliding glass door." I did not understand why he had it. I was sure he was going to sell it. Looking at where we lived, even at four years old, I understood there was no place to install such a luxurious item on our dilapidated old house. Seeing my confusion, he interjected, "I'm going to put this door in my new house."

In my four-year-old mind, I asked, "What new house?" Then I asked him the exact same question. He said to me, "The house that I'm going to have built one day." He told me that every day, he delivers these doors to these big, beautiful houses that these white folks are building in Jackson, Tennessee. Houses that once built, as a black man in the Democrat-controlled Jim Crow South, he would have to go to the back door when visiting. But today, he had bought himself one of those glass doors because one day he would have himself one of those homes, and that sliding glass door would be his back door.

I was like, "Yeah, whatever." See, black men were always talking about what they were going to do and never did anything. The fact that my father had acted was the only indication I had that he was any different.

We placed the glass door on the screened-in back porch, and my father laid down some rules for my three siblings and me: No roughhousing, throwing rocks, bumping into, or touching the glass door. We were never even allowed to open the box and expect the contents. Any violations meant stern retribution.

Years passed, and the box with the door in it sat there. It became a fixture on the back porch. The box, even though unopened, became mildewed, weather-beaten, and torn in places. But it remained intact.

Periodically I would see my father inspect the door, ensuring that it had not been tampered with. Sometimes I would witness him staring at it. I did not know whether it motivated or vexed him. I do know that as the years passed, it seemed as though my father was just another poor black man who was only a wishful braggart and nothing more.

A few years after the delivery of the door, my father started working for a wealthy black man in my hometown of Brownsville,

Tennessee, named Mr. Al Rawles. Mr. Rawles owned a life insurance company and a funeral home. My father worked for him collecting monthly payments on a debit route. In the 1960s, poor black people did not have checking accounts and seldom used the mail. Therefore, in order to collect his monthly fee from his thousands of black clients, Mr. Rawles hired dozens of trustworthy, good-looking, and articulate young black people to drive to the homes of his policyholders to collect their monthly payments.

It was a good job. My father started wearing a suit and tie to work with shiny shoes and didn't have to get dirty to make his money. This was strange for any man in the South during that time. Especially for a black man. Soon he became a manager. My father was on the rise.

One day out of the blue, almost five years later, which in the mind of a child is a lifetime, my father excitedly demanded that my brothers and I assist him in putting that glass door in the back of his truck. He said it needed to be measured. I did not know what that meant. He insisted we be extremely careful.

The box had become mildewed, tattered, and almost falling apart from time and exposure. Its condition was so fragile, while finally sliding it into the back of my father's truck, the box came apart, and for the first time in my life, I beheld the beauty and majesty of the sliding glass door. My brothers and I looked at each other, silent in total shock and amazement. Before we could say anything, my father sped off. I did not know where. I thought I'd never see the glass door again.

On July 4, 1861, Confederate Democrats were systematically murdering fellow citizens in an attempt to destroy the United States of America and establish a totalitarian nation spreading from the Mason-Dixon Line to Chile in South America. This

Democratic Party–controlled nation would be based on the lie of white supremacy and class. It would be would the first Nazi state. In an effort to thwart this calamity, on this day, Abraham Lincoln addressed Congress. He explained why it was essential that the United States be preserved, and that the Nazi state the Democrats had invented and sustained must be defeated. Lincoln said,

> This is essentially a people's contest. On the side of the Union it is a struggle for maintaining in the world that form and substance of government whose leading object is to elevate the condition of men; to lift artificial weights from all shoulders; to clear the paths of laudable pursuits for all; to afford all an unfettered start and fair chance in the race of life.

My father personified the concepts in Lincoln's speech: He "elevated" his condition. He lifted the "artificial weights" of class and race from his shoulders. He took the path toward the "laudable pursuits" of family, career, and private property. And as Thoreau said, he walked "confidently in the direction of his dreams."

Shakespeare said, "Our doubts are traitors and make us lose the good we oft might win by fearing to attempt." Faith is the opposite of doubt. My father has always had faith. President Lincoln spoke of this faith in his message to Congress on July 4, 1861, and my father acted on it, as we all must.

Hebrews 11:1 says, "Faith is the substance of things hoped for, the evidence of things not seen." To all of you young people who have succumbed to the Democratic Party line of racism, hatred, greed, envy, and victimization—please heed my father's story. With all the challenges directed at him, at eight years of age, he has never displayed any bitterness. My father, Ivory T. Ellison, did not wait for the government or the white man to affirm him. He aspired, saved, and planned. For his work in Brownsville, he has received citations from the Congress of the United States, the United States Senate, and the president of the United States.

Even though this Democratic Party Nazi state still exists, my father and I both understand that we are passing through this world. As we pass through it, we are obligated to love one another, help one another, and, as Christians, evangelize. The political Left and the Democratic Party have shrouded the world in darkness. It may get darker, still. But I am encouraged by the writings of the great C. S. Lewis. He said, "We live in the Shadowlands. The sun is always shining somewhere else. Round a bend in the road. Over the bough of a hill."

The Shadowlands Oneplace.com records Alex Dobson as saying during the Watchman Radio Hour:

> We live in the Shadowlands. This life will not last. There is suffering here. There is death. What we experience in this life is only temporary and behind the curtain is a life yet to come, the glory of which cannot be compared to this present world, in a way, it's all a mystery, but it is true.

But first, we must live. And there is no life without freedom and no freedom without courage. For this reason, God commanded us to "fear not." Conversely, for this reason, the political Left and the Democratic Party must sow fear among the people under their control.

I am a child of God. An heir of Jesus Christ and my Father's Son. As his faith in God sustains him, my faith in God sustains me. Therefore, I am inferior to no one, nor do I fear any man.

Manifesting his faith and courage, my father took me to the den on May 6, 1972, when he moved into his new brick home with bathrooms, running water, central heating, and a car porch. There, installed in his den, stood his beautiful sliding glass door, where it still stands today. He slid it open, closed it back, and said to me, "I told you I was going to build my house around it. Didn't I?" He did.

Now, find your glass door. And build your house around it.

ACKNOWLEDGMENTS

♣

Thanks to David Limbaugh, AJ Rice, Johanna Loeb, My Daughters.